DATE			
SEP 0 2 2008			
MAR 1 2011			

SLAVERY IN AMERICAN HISTORY

SLAVE UPRISINGS AND RUNAWAYS

FIGHTING FOR FREEDOM AND THE UNDERGROUND RAILROAD

ANN E. ESKRIDGE

FOREWORD BY SERIES ADVISOR DR. HENRY LOUIS GATES, JR.

Enslow Publishers, Inc.

40 Industrial Road   PO Box 38
Box 398   Aldershot
Berkeley Heights, NJ 07922   Hants GU12 6BP
USA   UK

http://www.enslow.com

Y 306.326

~~M⬛⬛⬛⬛⬛⬛⬛⬛⬛~~ **Acknowledgements**
This work could not have been completed without the generous assistance of University of Detroit Mercy, Professor of History, Roy Finkenbine, who lent me his knowledge as well as his books, and Christiana Paducci who assisted in research. My grateful thanks also goes out to the librarians at University of Detroit Mercy for making this book possible.

Library of Congress Cataloging-in-Publication Data

Eskridge, Ann E.
   Slave uprisings and runaways : fighting for freedom and the Underground Railroad/ Ann E. Eskridge.
      p. cm. — (Slavery in American history)
   Includes bibliographical references and index.
   ISBN-10: 0-7660-2154-8
   1. Slave insurrections—United States—Juvenile literature. 2. Fugitive slaves—United States—History—Juvenile literature. 3. Slaves—United States—Biography—Juvenile literature. 4. Slavery—United States—History—Juvenile literature. 5. Underground railroad—Juvenile literature. [1. Slave insurrections. 2. Fugitive slaves. 3. Slavery. 4. Underground railroad. 5. African Americans—Biography.] I. Title. II. Series.
   E447.E84   2004
   306.3'62'0973—dc22

                                          2003026533

ISBN-13: 978-0-7660-2154-9

Printed in the United States of America

10 9 8 7 6 5 4 3 2

To Our Readers: We have done our best to make sure all Internet Addresses in this book were active and appropriate when we went to press. However, the author and the publisher have no control over and assume no liability for the material available on those Internet sites or on other Web sites they may link to. Any comments or suggestions can be sent by e-mail to comments@enslow.com or to the address on the back cover.

Illustration Credits: The Art Archive, p. 59; Bridgeman photos, pp. 30, 76; Clipart.com, pp. 10, 19; Courtesy of the Association for the Study of African American Life and History, Inc., 1915 (ASALH) (formerly Association for the Study of Negro Life and History, Inc., (ASNLH), website: www.asalh.org, e-mail: asalh@earthlink.net, p. 37; Enslow Publishers, Inc., pp. 78, 89; Getty Images/Hulton Archive, pp. 14, 57, 100; © Jane Reed, Harvard News Office, p. 5; From *The Legend of John Brown* by Richard O. Boyer, copyright © 1973 by Richard O. Boyer. Used by permission of Alfred A. Knopf, a division of Random House, Inc., p. 38; The National Archives and Records Administration, pp. 87, 104; North Wind Picture Archives, pp. 3, 9, 21, 31, 48, 54; Ohio History, pp. 83, 107, From *A Pictorical History of the Negro in America* by Langston Hughes and Milton Meltzer, copyright © 1956, 1963 by Langston Hughes and Milton Meltzer. © 1968 by Milton Meltzer and The Estate of Langston Hughes. Used by permission of Crown Publishers, a division of Random House, Inc., pp. 16–17; Picture History, p. 47; Reproduced from the Collections of the Library of Congress, pp. 1, 25, 44, 64, 70, 74, 92; Reproduced from the *Dictionary of American Portraits*, published by Dover Publications, Inc., 1967, pp. 51, 68.

Cover Illustration: Enslow Publishers, Inc. (Background); North Wind Picture Archives (Runaway slaves).

CONTENTS

American Slavery's Undying Legacy

While the Thirteenth Amendment outlawed slavery in the United States in 1865, the impact of that institution continued to be felt long afterward, and in many ways is still being felt today. The broad variety of experiences encompassed within that epoch of American history can be difficult to encapsulate. Enslaved, free, owner, trader, abolitionist: each "category" hides a complexity of experience as varied as the number of individuals who occupied these identities.

One thing is certain: in spite of how slavery has sometimes been portrayed, very few, if any, enslaved blacks were utter victims who quietly and passively accepted such circumstances. Those who claimed ownership over Africans and African Americans used violence, intimidation, and other means to wield a great degree of power and control. But as human beings—and as laborers within an economic system that depended on labor—all enslaved blacks retained varying degrees of agency within that system.

The "Slavery in American History" series provides a strong and needed overview of the most important aspects of American slavery, from the first transport of African slaves to the American colonies, to the long fight for abolition, to the lasting impact of slavery on America's economy, politics, and culture. Only by understanding American slavery and its complex legacies can we begin to understand the challenge facing not just African Americans, but all Americans: To make certain that our country is a living and breathing embodiment of the principles enunciated in the Constitution of the United States. Only by understanding the past can we mend the present and ensure the rights of our future generations.

—**Henry Louis Gates, Jr.,** *Ph.D., W.E.B. Du Bois Professor of the Humanities, Chair of the Department of African and African-American Studies, Director of the W.E.B. Du Bois Institute for African and African-American Research, Harvard University.*

Dr. Henry Louis Gates, Jr., Series Advisor

Dr. Henry Louis Gates, Jr., is author of a number of books including: *The Trials of Phillis Wheatley: America's First Poet and Her Encounters with the Founding Fathers*; *The African-American Century* (with Cornel West); *Little Known Black History Facts*; *Africana: The Encyclopedia of the African American Experience*; *Wonders of the African World*; *The Future of The Race* (with Cornel West); *Colored People: A Memoir*; *Loose Cannons: Notes on the Culture Wars*; *The Signifying Monkey: Towards A Theory of Afro-American Literary Criticism*; *Figures in Black: Words, Signs, and the Racial Self*; and *Thirteen Ways of Looking at a Black Man*.

Professor Gates earned his M.A. and Ph.D. in English Literature from Clare College at the University of Cambridge. Before beginning his work at Harvard in 1991, he taught at Yale, Cornell, and Duke universities. He has been named one of *Time* magazine's "25 Most Influential Americans," received a National Humanities Medal, and was elected to the American Academy of Arts and Letters.

When the first Africans stepped foot on North American soil in the spring of 1526, they began to work on Spanish sugar cane plantations in what is now South Carolina.[1] This colony failed. Historian Herbert Aptheker believes that these slaves staged the first rebellion on American soil, killing some of their masters and fleeing.[2] The Africans who escaped were helped by American Indians. By the end of the summer, the remaining colonists packed up and left.

Jamestown

A Dutch vessel sailed into Jamestown, Virginia, in 1619, and part of the essential cargo it brought to the first permanent English settlement was twenty Africans. Along with Europeans, these Africans were put to work in the fertile Virginia fields to raise tobacco, a cash crop, or they were used as servants in the household.

According to historian Edward Countryman, these Africans were not considered slaves. They might have been indentured servants just like the whites that worked beside them in the fields.[3] An indentured servant is one who enters into a contract to work off a debt. Usually, this contract was made with the captain of the ship sailing to Virginia. Instead of buying passage on the ship with money, the indentured servant purchased his passage with his labor. The captain would sell the contract to the highest bidder when he reached his destination. After working off his debt, the indentured servant would then buy land, participate in settlement life, and raise a family.

However, Africans were not uniformly treated as equals with other indentured servants. The Africans who came to Jamestown did not sign contracts that obliged them to work off their indebtedness nor did they cross the ocean voluntarily. Most of them had been captured.

Atlantic Creoles

There was another group of Africans who came to the colonies—the Atlantic Creoles. Although slaves, they became a valuable asset because of their ability to bridge the European and African worlds.[4] These Africans, who were of mixed heritage, lived on the western coast of Africa. They were a people who spoke several languages, were skilled in trade, and who possessed the ability to understand the culture and customs of both African tribes and European traders. They were settled in New Netherlands—today part of New York.

According to historian Ira Berlin, these African Creoles had the ability to, "integrate themselves into mainland society."[5] They understood what it took to "get along" and they used it to their advantage. Some Atlantic Creoles abandoned their own African beliefs and became Christians. They hoped that their conversion would better their chances of freedom and that their freedom would be passed on to their children. "By the middle of the seventeenth century, black people participated in almost every aspect of life in

New Netherland," Berlin writes.[6] Some of them had won their freedom and owned land and slaves too.

Early Emancipations

Africans needed to be able to understand and use the system in order to gain certain privileges—including his or her freedom. Their owners may have found their good character and loyalty worthy of special consideration—and thus, manumitted them—legally freeing them. They may have converted to Christianity and petitioned for their freedom. They may have even gone to court and argued for their right to be legally free. Their status depended on how well they were able to assimilate within the community.

The Growth of Slavery

The colonizing countries like England, Portugal, the Netherlands, France, and Spain were realizing tremendous profits from the cultivation of tobacco, sugar, and rice in their colonies. They wanted to make more money, but to do that, they needed more labor. It became a vicious cycle. More slaves were needed to grow more crops. With more crops there was the desire for more slaves.

There were arguments both for and against slavery at that time, but those for slavery had a stronger voice. Less than fifty years after 1619, there were three hundred Africans in Virginia. Two thousand Africans made up 5 percent of the Virginia population by 1671.[7] This rise was due

Slaves sometimes had their own prayer meetings. Many slaves converted to Christianity because they felt they would have a better chance of obtaining their freedom.

to the growth of the plantation system in the South and the need for trade labor in the North.

The first Africans used the system and the personal relationships with their owners to achieve a better, free life. It would be more difficult for future generations of slaves.

As more slaves arrived to support the growing colonial economy, the need to control them became greater. Slave laws were passed in the colonies, and slavery was officially legalized. Although these laws differed from one colony to another, the overall effect was to reinforce the status of Africans as slaves.

Slavery—A Way of Life

By the 1700s, the colonists were used to African and African-American labor. By 1790 there were 757,208 blacks in colonial America: 697,681 were slaves and 59,527 were free, according to author William Switala.[8] As an example of this population explosion, historian Ira Berlin notes that from 1700 to 1710 in Philadelphia, slaves made up one sixth of the population in that city.[9]

Africans and African Americans who gained their freedom and slaves worked in the cities as servants, craftsmen, farmers, ironworkers, shipbuilders, and sailors. In Philadelphia, 17–22 percent of seafaring jobs went to blacks. In fact, the maritime trade often offered better opportunities to black men in Atlantic coastal cities.[10]

In the 1700s, Africans and African Americans had all kinds of jobs.

Slaves also toiled in the fields. In the North, they may have worked alongside their master or white indentured servants and did a variety of jobs. As the plantation economy grew, slaves grew tobacco in Maryland and Virginia, rice in South Carolina and Georgia, and sugarcane in lower Mississippi.

Slave Codes

The colonists also viewed slaves as a threat to their safety. In some places, slaves and free black people outnumbered white colonists.

To control the growing slave and free black population, colonial governments began passing laws to govern the movement and behavior of blacks. For example, in Virginia in 1669, a slave law was passed that outlawed a slave from carrying any kind of weapon, while laws about how masters could treat slaves were more lenient.[11] A Virginia law made it a non-criminal offense for a master to kill a slave in the process of "correcting" him—punishing him.[12] Other colonial laws prevented slaves from gathering in large numbers, walking without a master present, intermarrying, or striking a white person even in self-defense.

The state of Louisiana was concerned about its growing free black population. In 1724, it adopted a code that required manumitted slaves "to defer to their former owners. It punished free black people more than whites and barred interracial marriage."[13]

The punishment for violating these laws ranged from

lashings to imprisonment, and even death. Collectively, these laws that governed the life of slaves were called slave codes. These slave codes were meant to prevent slaves from running away or rebelling.

A Moral Question

The fear of rebellions became greater as the colonists themselves were straining under restrictive laws imposed by England. The American colonists were resisting England's control over them and the colonists were willing to fight to gain their independence from England. Because of this, the question of slavery became an increasingly moral one to some. On one hand, the founding fathers of the Declaration of Independence declared that, "all men are created equal."[14] And yet, many of them owned slaves. Some signers like Benjamin Franklin championed the end of slavery. But in order to get all thirteen colonies to sign the Declaration of Independence, any mention of freeing slaves or condemning slavery was omitted from the document.

The signers of the Declaration of Independence believed that they were, ". . . endowed by their Creator with certain unalienable Rights, that among these are Life, Liberty and the pursuit of Happiness. . . . "[15] And the colonies waged war to gain the same rights that they were denying the slaves.

Slave Soldiers

Slaves wanted their freedom too and many believed the Revolutionary War would help them win it. Slaves fought on both sides, British and Colonial, hoping that whoever won would set them free. For instance, Virginia's Governor Lord Dunmore offered slaves freedom in return for their military service to fight for the British.[16]

After the Revolutionary War, some slaves were set free, set sail with the British back to England, or used the opportunity during the war to escape. But many were returned to slavery.

A Southern Slave Culture

By the end of the 1700s, the newly formed United States may have been united in the cause of freedom, but they were still divided over the issue of slavery. Gradually, however, Northern states passed their own emancipation acts.[17] Vermont became the first state to free its slaves in 1777. A slave could also be privately manumitted by his owner. By

SOURCE DOCUMENT

I was with him in the war, and helped to scalp and kill many Indians, which I now exceedingly regret, as they were innocent and defenceless [sic], and were fast tending to a condition not much better than my own. I was with him through the whole course of the Revolutionary War.[18]

James Roberts was a slave from Maryland who fought alongside his owner, Colonel Francis De Shields, in the Revolutionary War. However, Roberts did not earn his freedom by participating in battle and went back to work for De Shields at the close of the war.

1776, there were sixty thousand free blacks or approximately 8 percent of the national black population.[19] Still each state had laws designed to control these newly freed slaves.

In the South, however, a new invention allowed farmers to harvest more cotton in less time. Called the cotton gin, it increased the popularity of cotton growing. Cotton would eventually become the South's most important crop. According to the United States National Archives and Records Administration:

> Cotton growing became so profitable for the planters that it greatly increased their demand for both land and slave labor. . . . From 1790 until Congress banned the importation

Cotton picking was hard work. Many slaves suffered from aching backs, bleeding fingers, and dehydration after a long day in the fields.

of slaves from Africa in 1808, Southerners imported 80,000 Africans. By 1860 approximately one in three Southerners was a slave.[20]

During that same period, Congress passed the 1793 Fugitive Slave Act, which allowed slaveholders to retrieve runaway slaves in free states. At the same time, Canada passed its own Emancipation Act, which outlawed the importation of Africans to Canada and also outlawed American slaveholders from coming into Canada and retrieving runaway slaves.

By the end of the 1700s slavery was growing in the South and being gradually eliminated in the North.

The Haitian Revolution

The French Revolution began in 1789. The lower classes overthrew the aristocratic classes and the French monarchy. That uprising also helped spark another rebellion just a doorstep away from America—the Haitian Revolution.

In that revolution, mixed-race and African slaves in Saint Domingue successfully overthrew the colonial French government on the island and founded the country of Haiti in 1804. Haiti would be governed by former slaves.[21] Some refugees who fled the Haitian revolution migrated to America where they brought back horror stories of violence and mayhem; stories about how slaves had revolted and won their independence.

Although most slaves in America could not read, many of them were influenced by these world events. They wanted their freedom too.

UPRISINGS

S LAVE RESISTANCE RANGED FROM SABOTAGING equipment, being outwardly defiant, slowing the pace of work and running away; to violence against masters and outright rebellion.

What Caused an Uprising?

The first known rebellion took place when the first slaves landed on North American soil in 1526. The last known rebellion was being planned as the Civil War was raging. A slave conspiracy was uncovered in 1861 in Mississippi.[1] Historian Herbert Aptheker believes these uprisings had a pattern:

> The uprisings and plots came in waves, as though anger accumulated and vented itself and then a period of rest and recuperation was needed before the next upsurge.[2]

What made one slave run away and another slave lead a rebellion is as much a part of the slave's character as his circumstance and the choices he made.

Historian Eugene Genovese writes that certain factors needed to exist in order to spark a rebellion. Among these factors were: black population density, whether slaves were African born, and whether slaves outnumbered whites in a particular area.[3]

Uprisings took place more frequently when slaves outnumbered the white populations. In cities like Charleston, South Carolina, slaves made up a majority of the population.

Rebellion was much more common where slaves were in concentrated numbers and where one plantation was close to another. Slave populations outside of the cities were for the most part scattered, particularly as more people began to move farther west in search of virgin soil for farming. But during the Louisiana Rebellion of 1811, slaves traveled from one nearby plantation to another, gathering strength as they went.

Being African born as opposed to born into slavery was another condition that scholars suggest may have contributed to rebellion. Those who remembered their cultural and religious beliefs were more likely to rebel as opposed to those born into slavery.

New York Riots and Rebellions
There was a heavy concentration of slaves and freemen living in close communication with each other on the island of Manhattan. And living in this close-knit community were first-generation slaves—slaves who still had an African belief system. These slaves began to plot their escape.[4]

On April 1, some twenty blacks set fire to a building and the fire spread. While the whites were trying to put out the blaze, the slaves attacked. Nine whites were shot, beaten, or stabbed to death and six more were wounded.

Some of the rioters were caught, tried, and executed.

> . . . In that Court were twenty seven condemned whereof twenty one were executed, one being a woman with child, her execution by that meanes suspended, some were burnt others hanged, one broke on the wheele, and one hung a live in chains in the town, so that there has been the most exemplary punishment inflicted. . .
>
> Governor Robert Hunter to
> The Lords of Trade, June 23, 1712[5]

After this riot, stricter laws were put in place that regulated even more the movement of slaves. One law in particular restricted newly freed slaves from owning land or property.[6] But there was rumor of another rebellion in New York in 1741 when a series of suspicious fires spread throughout the city. In fact, there were rumors and whisperings of uprisings in almost every colony. Reports of slaves poisoning masters, slaves taking up arms, fighting, and plotting flourished. Any hint of slave unrest brought repercussions, and a full-blown rebellion was met with quick action and brute force.[7]

The Stono Rebellion

Blacks were in the majority in South Carolina during the 1730s, because cultivating rice—the main crop then—was so labor intensive. According to historian Roy Finkenbine, "By 1739, blacks outnumbered whites nearly two to one among the colony's 56,000 inhabitants."[8] Finkenbine writes that many of these slaves had been recently imported from Africa and worked on large plantations where there were absentee landlords. In Florida, just one state away, the Spanish government who then owned that colony encouraged slaves to run away, convert to Catholicism, and take up arms to defend the Spanish colony against the British. Once slaves made it to Florida, it was hard for their former masters to get them back. Because of this, a group of slaves in South Carolina decided to run away to Florida. This sparked the Stono Rebellion.

The group started out numbering twenty on the morning of September 9, 1739. But it grew as the band of slaves, beating drums, marched along the Stono River. They burned plantations, killed slave owners, and freed other slaves, trying to reach Fort Mose in St. Augustine, Florida.

A hundred slaves in all were estimated to have participated at the height of the rebellion just outside of Charleston, South Carolina. An anonymous letter describing the incident was reprinted in English newspapers. It described the initial rioters as being twenty-one Angolans.

. . . they calling out Liberty, marched on with Colours displayed, and two Drums beating, pursing all the white

In the 1700s, slaves in South Carolina mostly worked on rice plantations.

people they met with, and killing Man Woman and Child when they could come up to them.[9]

Later that afternoon white planters and state militia arrived and opened fire. Sixty people were killed, most of whom were slaves. But this riot changed the way South Carolina's whites supervised their slaves. The state assembly enacted more slave codes. They also limited the number of new slaves that could come into the colony, thereby reducing the ratio of blacks to whites. The assembly also tried to eliminate escape routes to Florida. They increased slave patrols on well-traveled routes. They also tried to

. . . one of the most effectual means that could be used at present to prevent such desertion of our Negroes is to encourage some Indians by a suitable reward to pursue and if possible to bring back the Deserters, and while the Indians are thus employed they would be in the way ready to intercept others that might attempt to follow and I have sent for the Chiefs of the Chickasaws living at New Windsor and the Catawbaw Indians for that purpose. . . .[10]

Lieutenant Governor William Bull wrote to Great Britain's Board of Trade on October 5, 1739, asking it to reward any American Indian who helped kill or capture fugitives of the Stono Rebellion.

run the Spanish out of Florida as punishment for harboring fugitive slaves.[11]

With every act of rebellion or rumor of uprising came increased patrols and stricter laws governing the movement of slaves and free African Americans. But no matter how restrictive these laws were, there were always slaves determined to be free or die trying. And this was an individual choice that each slave made.

A SLAVE REBELS

BORN IN VIRGINIA IN 1776, GABRIEL, WHOSE master's name was Prosser, was an unlikely leader for a rebellion. He seemed to have more than most slaves—and the most to lose. He was married. He had learned how to read and write at a young age. He was a skilled tradesman –a blacksmith. Reading, writing, and being a blacksmith gave him a certain status in the slave community.[1] He was also a hire-out; a slave who is hired by other people, thus earning more money for his master and in some cases himself.[2]

Gabriel, like other hire-outs, found opportunities for his skills because Virginia was growing economically. Before the Revolutionary War the major crop in Virginia was tobacco; now it was wheat. This required a different farming structure. Slaves performed all sorts of tasks and planters hired their slaves out by the year, month, day, or

job.[3] This gave slaves a freedom of movement that they may
have not experienced before.

Yearning for Freedom

As a twenty-one-year-old hire-out in Richmond, Virginia,
just before the turn of the century, Gabriel would have been
able to associate with freemen and whites, skilled trades-
men and merchants.[4] His freedom to move among different
segments of society may have given him ideas.

One day Gabriel got into trouble for trying to steal a pig.
In the process, he bit off part of a white man's ear. He was
branded on his hand as punishment for this offense. He
was put in jail again when the man he had injured thought
that Gabriel was still a threat to him. Only after Gabriel's
owner assured the court that his slave would not get into
trouble and posted his bond, was Gabriel released. But
Gabriel wanted true freedom; and freedom for all slaves.

Gabriel's Plan

Gabriel hatched a complicated plot that involved slaves and
free blacks. They would take over Capitol Square in
Richmond and hold Virginia Governor James Monroe as a
hostage to bargain for the freedom of Virginia slaves. He
hoped that poor whites and American Indians would rally
around his cause and help. Gabriel and his followers
recruited men from the small towns around Richmond
and even some slaves from the country. According to
court testimony at his trial, Gabriel and his men plotted

Gabriel Prosser's rebels planned to kidnap Governor James Monroe (pictured).

the conspiracy at every occasion where slaves gathered:

> The swords made by the prisoners were to be distributed by . . . Gabriel; swords have been making ever since last Harvest. 1,000 men was to be raised from Richmond, 600 from Ground Squirrel Bridge, and 400 from Goochland. Meetings were frequently held at William Young's under pretext of attending preachment, and at other times--viz., at Fish feast and at Barbacues, to concert the plan of Insurrection.[5]

According to trial witnesses, hundreds of men were involved in the plot. By August of 1800, Gabriel and his men were ready to put his plan in motion. And on August 30, they were ready to move, but that day there was a storm so fierce that it threatened to wash away bridges and roads that were necessary for the revolt.

Caught!

The rebellion was postponed until the next day, but when the time came, the plan had been found out and white

My brother Gabriel was the person who influenced me to join him and others in order that (as he said) we might conquer the white people and possess ourselves of their property. I enquired how we were to effect it. He said by falling upon them (the whites) in the dead of night, at which time they would be unguarded and unsuspicious. . . . he applied to me to make scythe-swords . . . [6]

Gervas Storrs and Joseph Seldon wrote down the confession of Solomon, Gabriel's brother. Storrs and Seldon were officials of the court. Solomon was found guilty and hanged the next day.

patrols roamed the countryside looking for the rebels. Gabriel disappeared. Thirty slaves were captured and held for trial. By September when the trials started, Gabriel and one of his key men were still in hiding.

The full size and scope of the rebellion was revealed during the trial. Slaves turned against slaves as they tried to save themselves from the gallows. In the meantime, Gabriel attempted to escape by boarding a schooner. The captain of the ship was willing to help him. But when they got into Norfolk, Virginia, a slave alerted the authorities. Gabriel and the captain of the ship were arrested.

Gabriel went on trial in October. Witnesses testified against him and he was hanged on October 10. Twenty-six slaves were hanged in Richmond. Some others were captured and hanged in other parts of Virginia.

Charles Deslondes

Eleven years after Gabriel's Conspiracy, a deadly rebellion involving three hundred to five hundred slaves took place in 1811 in Louisiana. It was led by Charles Deslondes, a Haitian-born slave. Although this was the largest known slave revolt on United States soil, there is not much information on Deslondes or specific details of the plot. But people described the rebellion as a "miniature Haiti."[7]

What historians do know is that the Louisiana plantations were in close proximity to each other, aiding Deslondes in gathering more rebels. He led a group of insurgents down River Road toward New Orleans, burning plantations along the way. Two whites were killed, crops were burned, and ammunition and weapons were stolen.

Louisiana planters, free black militia, and the United States Army confronted the rebelling slaves. Sixty-six slaves were killed; some were captured and sentenced to death. Those who were sentenced to death were decapitated and their heads stuck on poles along the same road where the slaves revolted, as a warning to other slaves. But that did not stop another black man from plotting his rebellion— this time in Charleston, South Carolina.

A FREE PERSON REBELS

PLANTERS WERE CONCERNED ABOUT THE growing free black population. According to historical writer, Alonford James Robinson Jr., between 1800 and 1810, the free black population in the United States nearly doubled from 108,395 to 186,446. And by the Civil War in 1860, free blacks numbered close to five hundred thousand.[1]

New Orleans' free black population by 1803 numbered almost eighteen hundred. One fifth of the city's population was of African descent.[2]

Free Blacks

Freemen were either born into freedom, had successfully petitioned for their freedom, bought their freedom, ran away to freedom, or were manumitted.[3] Free people of color were technically free, even though they did not have rights equal to whites. These rights varied from state to state. In some states a free person could vote or attend school, while in other states voting was outlawed and attending public school was forbidden.[4]

Some of the free blacks were politically active in the abolitionist movement—a movement to free the slaves. Many worked to improve the conditions of slaves, and some were wealthy. The fact that these free blacks could serve as role models for other slaves and were willing to support the end of slavery made slave owners uneasy. Many free blacks were harassed. Some American leaders thought of a way to lessen the free black population.

The American Colonization Society

As one solution to the growing population of free people, the American Colonization Society (ACS) was formed in 1816 by Presbyterian ministers. These white men felt that it was best that free people of color emigrate—be exported—to Africa where they might have a better life living unrestricted under their own form of government and among other blacks. The members of the ACS felt that this would be the best way to help blacks because they believed that blacks could never participate successfully in American life. Some of the more prominent members of the ACS included: Henry Clay, James Monroe, and Francis Scott Key.[5] The ACS thought that this was a charitable way of helping those who had suffered at the hands of slavery and who now were free. Many whites supported this view. But many freemen took angry exception to it, believing that the

ACS's attempt to urge free blacks to go back to Africa only disguised its racist views, according to writer Alonford James Robinson, Jr.[6]

By this time in the country, many of the free African Americans had been born in the United States—not Africa. They felt that they had every right to remain in this country and that the idea of sending them back to Africa was just another way of avoiding the real issue of abolishing slavery and making blacks equal to whites. In an open letter, free African Americans made their case to the ACS:

> We are natives of the United States; our ancestors were brought to this country by means over which they had no

Even though many blacks objected to the American Colonization Society, some decided that going to Liberia was better than living in the United States. These refugees are on their way to Liberia.

The American Colonization Society succeeded in having the colony of Liberia established for relocated African Americans. The colony's capital was named Monrovia, after President James Monroe.

control; we have our attachments to the soil, and we feel that we have rights in common with other Americans . . .[7]

Still, the ACS helped emigrate between twelve thousand to twenty thousand African Americans. Many of them populated the British colony of Liberia.[8]

Those Who Remained

But the growing number of freemen continued to alarm whites because the very presence of free blacks seemed to undermine the arguments slaveholders made for continuing the institution. Many of these free blacks were well-off, educated, hardworking, and law-abiding citizens. Some even owned slaves—often family members who were bought so they could be protected.

Freemen were suspected of helping slaves run away or they were suspected of conspiring with slaves to incite rebellion. In some cases this was true, particularly in South Carolina in 1822.

At that time, free blacks and slaves outnumbered whites in Charleston, South Carolina. Free blacks in the city were highly skilled.[9] They were shopkeepers, house servants, carpenters, and longshoremen. One of these free African Americans was Denmark Vesey.

A Slave Named Denmark

Much of what we know about Denmark Vesey comes from the testimony of others at his trial. He was either born in the Caribbean or Africa. He lived in the Caribbean as a young child. But he was born into slavery and eventually became the property of slaver Captain Joseph Vesey.[10] As property, he sailed with Captain Vesey to different countries. The slave boy Denmark was said to be clever and intelligent. Captain Vesey sold him to a planter in Saint Dominigue, Haiti, when he was a teenager. Haiti was a harsh place for slaves. Planting and harvesting sugar was back-breaking work and many slaves died. On Captain Vesey's next trip to Haiti, the planter who had bought the boy, Denmark, wanted to sell him back to Vesey because Denmark had epileptic seizures in the field—he was considered damaged. Some historians believe Denmark pretended to have "fits" to get out of a harsh situation.[11]

Vesey bought the boy back and made him his personal

servant. During the times that he traveled with the captain, Vesey was exposed to all the horrors of slavery. And either through gossip or firsthand accounts, he heard of the unrest, rebellion, and revolutions on the world stage. It was said that he spoke different languages and he was literate.

When Captain Vesey decided to settle in Charleston, Denmark went with him. And there, through luck, he won a lottery of fifteen hundred dollars. With six hundred dollars, he bought his freedom.[12] He then established himself as a carpenter in Charleston.

Reverend Vesey

As a free person and a carpenter whose skill was sought by many, Denmark Vescy was able to move in various social classes. He helped establish a separate black African Methodist Episcopal Church (AME) and became a church leader.[13] This church was constantly being monitored by whites. His intelligence, his awareness of world events, his skill in reading and writing, and his status as a free person of color established him in the black community. Like Gabriel before him, those were the very qualities that made him someone who was a leader . . . and rebel.

According to court testimony, the passages that Denmark Vesey read from the Bible to the black Methodist congregation were not those of "turning the other cheek." Instead, he quoted passages from the Old Testament, comparing the enslavement of Jews by Pharaoh to the enslavement of Africans. He gathered around him men he could trust. With them, he planned to take over the city of Charleston and its arsenals.

A Plot to Capture Charleston

For years, Vesey planned his rebellion in secret, aided by Gullah Jack, an African born slave and priest. Jack was said to have magical powers and intimidated and inspired other African slaves to join the planned revolt.

Vesey recruited from the ranks of trusted house servants and rough longshoremen, from slaves on plantations to freemen in the city.[14] Vesey then gave the word that the rebellion would take place in June 1822.

With hundreds of people involved in the plot, inevitably his plan was found out. Vesey changed the date of the uprising, but before one shot was fired, the plot leaked out again. The authorities learned about the rebellion through several slave informants. According to court documents:

> . . . the next day, Friday the 14th, [he] came to his master, and informed him . . . that a public disturbance was contemplated by the blacks, and not a moment should be lost in informing the . . . authorities . . .[15]

The streets of Charleston were filled with soldiers and militia ready to put down any uprising.

One by one, Vesey's conspirators were arrested. He was captured after being sought for two days. The details of the plot shocked many because it was likely that Vesey and his rebels were planning to kill men, women, and children. According to information from Jesse, an informant:

. . . they intended to make the attack by setting the governor's mills on fire, and also some houses near the water, and as soon as the bells began to ring for fire, that they should kill every man, as he came out of his door, . . . and that it should be done with axes and clubs, and afterwards they should murder the women and children for he said, God had so chmmanded (sic) it in the Scriptures.[16]

Rebellion or No Rebellion?

On June 28, the court sentenced Vesey to death. He was executed on the morning of July 2. That morning, five slaves were hanged with Vesey. Thirty-five slaves were hanged in all, and forty-three slaves were exiled.

But historian Michael Johnson believes that the conspiracy "was not about to happen; that Denmark Vesey and the other men sentenced to hang or be sold into exile were not guilty of organizing an insurrection . . ."[17] He believes that the witnesses were intimidated into testifying in order to support the white community's fears of a black conspiracy. Other historians tend to disagree with Johnson about the validity of the conspiracy. Neither Vesey nor his closest co-conspirators ever talked, so there is no firsthand information.

Regardless of whether or not the uprising was more fiction than fact, laws governing the movement of African Americans in the South became stricter. The authorities were on constant alert. The AME church where Vesey belonged was eventually burned down.[18]

Despite these restrictions, eleven years later a slave preacher carried out another rebellion that horrified the South.

VISIONARY OR
MADMAN?

MOST OF THE INFORMATION ABOUT REBEL leader Nat Turner is supplied to us by his "biographer" Thomas Gray, also his court-appointed attorney. Gray wrote down Turner's confession while Turner awaited his execution in 1831. Like that of the Vesey uprising, the accuracy of this information is being questioned by historians since no other information supports these confessions. But Gray's book, *Confessions of Nat Turner*, has been used by historians to interpret who Nat Turner was. Some historians have described him as a glorious rebel leader, fighting against the institution of slavery. Others paint him as a delusional madman who used the issue of slavery to go on a killing spree.[1]

Turner's Story

The following account of Nat Turner's life, even though taken from many sources, originates from Gray's book.

The quotes are all in Turner's voice since he was telling Gray his story.

Born a slave in 1800, Nat Turner told Gray that his family and other slaves considered him a prophet. He seemed to be able to retell events that happened before his birth. He also seemed to be able to predict the future and read and write without ever having been taught. In his teen years, he studied the Bible, fasted, and prayed. He also had visions.

A Vision

In 1821, at twenty-one years old, Turner ran away from his owner only to return a month later because a vision he had told him to. Three years later, in 1824, he had his second vision. He saw lights in the sky and . . .

> then I found on the leaves in the woods hieroglyphic characters and numbers, with the forms of men in different attitudes, portrayed in blood, and representing the figures I had seen before in the heavens.[2]

Nat Turner was a preacher and was considered to be a visionary by some of his fellow slaves.

A third vision came to Turner. It was very specific: "arise and prepare myself and slay my enemies with their own weapons."[3]

But the sign he was waiting for did not come until three years later in February 1831. It came in the form of a solar eclipse. He then confided his plan to four men and they decided they would act on July 4; the birthday of the nation. But on July 4, Turner fell ill and so they waited until another atmospheric disturbance happened on August 13. That day the sun turned an unnatural bluish-green. And now Turner believed that this was the last sign he needed.

A Rebel Force Grows

August 21, 1831, Turner and six men ate dinner in the woods. At 2 A.M., they set out for Turner's owner's house.

Nat Turner (center with beard) and the initial group of rebels met in the woods near a place called Cabin Pond.

SOURCE DOCUMENT

A dog in the neighborhood passing by my hiding-place one night while I was out, was attracted by some meat I had in my cave, and crawled in and stole it, and was coming out just as I returned. A few nights after, two Negroes having started to go hunting with the same dog, and passed that way, the dog came again to the place, and having just gone out to walk about, discovered me and barked . . . [4]

Nat Turner describes how his hiding place in the woods was found.

Turner had been sold to a Joseph Travis. He liked his new owner and thought him kind, but that did not stop him and his men from killing Travis and his family in their sleep. [5]

The original six rebels grew to forty as they went from house to house killing the whites who lived there. All tolled, Turner's men succeeded in killing fifty-five white people. Several thousand troops and groups of vigilantes converged on the area. Nat Turner escaped and remained on the run for two months, finally being captured on October 30.

Turner's "Confession"

While in jail, Turner spoke to Thomas Gray. Gray wrote that Turner believed God inspired him.

Turner was hanged on November 11 and then skinned.

Even though there were approximately forty Turner rebels, almost fifty-five blacks were executed for their alleged participation and two hundred more—as far away as North Carolina—were murdered by white mobs. Historian Kenneth Greenberg notes that the story of Nat Turner is "far more a tale of the death of slaves than of masters."[6]

After the rebellion, the Virginia Legislature considered abolishing slavery. The grandson of Thomas Jefferson introduced a bill that would gradually emancipate slaves born after 1840. But the bill eventually was defeated. Instead, the legislature decided on more restrictive and oppressive laws against slaves and free people.

Historians agree that Turner's Rebellion had an impact for decades throughout the South. Not until white abolitionist John Brown gained notoriety, was there a comparable controversial antislavery figure.

REBELLION AT SEA

T HE IMPORTATION OF SLAVES INTO THE UNITED States was banned in 1808. This meant that no new slaves could be brought into the country.

Slaves at Sea

Even after the ban, slave traders still smuggled in slaves using a variety of deceptions. This is what happened to Cinque, an African from the Mende country on the West Coast of Africa.[1]

Cinque and his countrymen revolted at sea. It was one of several hundred revolts that either took place on African soil against ships or during the transatlantic voyage to the New World. After examining European shipping records and *Lloyd's List* for insurance claims and losses, historian David Richardson has figured that there were, "485 acts of violence by Africans against slave ships and their crews. These include ninety-three instances of attacks from the shore by apparently 'free' Africans against ships or longboats and 392 cases of shipboard revolts by slaves."[2] According to Richardson at least 90 percent of these attacks or 353 happened between 1698–1807.[3]

Captains of slave ships were well aware that an insurrection might be possible. They took measures against attacks by shackling the Africans, making sure there were plenty of firearms and ammunition on board, and keeping guard over their captives.

Ships that loaded in certain locations in Africa seemed to have more revolts than those ships loading in other regions. According to Richardson:

Overall, rebellions on ships going to places north of the Gold Coast and to Gabon-Cape Lopez were about four times more common than one might expect from their share of slave shipments from Atlantic Africa to the Americas.[4]

Other factors Richardson believes contributed to ship revolts include the proportion of male to female slaves, tribal make-up of the slaves, ship management, and crew sickness.

Even though rebellion on board or on the African shores resulted in loss of life, Richardson estimates that "disease was far more costly than revolt to shippers of slaves."[5]

However, he believes that shipboard revolts did change the slave trade. Because of these revolts, there were fewer Africans captured and imported as slaves to the New World.

This is because it was too expensive to arm and defend a slave ship.

Cinque

What we know of Cinque's background comes from his court testimony. According to that, Cinque's African name was Sengbe Pieh and he was kidnapped in January 1839 and forced to march ten days to the coast where he was loaded, along with several hundred other captured Africans, onto a slave schooner bound for Cuba.[6]

The Africans landed near Havana and were sold on the open market. This is where his name was changed to Joseph Cinque. The Africans were given Spanish names and called "Black *ladinos*"—slaves who had lived long enough in the country to speak the language and know the customs.[7] This was a trick used to disguise the fact that they were newly arriving slaves. Cinque and fifty-two other members of the Mende tribe were sold to Jose Ruiz and Pedro Montez, who planned to resell them in Cuba.

Mutiny on the *Amistad*

In June, Ruiz and Montez along with the slaves boarded the schooner *Amistad* to sail down the Cuban coast. Once on the water, the Africans broke free of their chains, led by Cinque. They took weapons like machetes and waited until dawn to attack the captain and his three crewmen. Cinque killed the captain, but two of the crew escaped. The third crew member, a cabin boy who was a ladino, was left unharmed. Montez' and Ruiz' lives were spared only

Cinque and the other rebels made weapons that resembled machetes. A machete is a type of large knife.

because they promised to steer the ship back to Africa. By day, the two hostages would steer the ship east to Africa and by night they steered it back toward the United States, hoping to steer the schooner to a friendly port.

By August 1839, the ship *Amistad* was caught and taken to New London, Connecticut, where Montez and Ruiz told authorities that the Africans had revolted and murdered crew members.[8] The Africans could not speak English or Spanish so they could not defend themselves. But they were brought to federal court and a trial date was set.

The Trial

The Spanish ambassador appealed to United States president Martin Van Buren to return the ship and the Africans. The ambassador argued that any punishment of the Africans should be done by Spanish law. The President agreed because he did not want to alienate his southern political support. It was an election year and he was running for a second term.

But three abolitionists—people who wanted to free the slaves—intervened and formed a supporting committee. They obtained legal counsel for the Africans and found a translator who was able to tell the Africans' stories: how they had been kidnapped and brought to Cuba illegally. This became the basis of their testimony at the trial, which began on January 7, 1840.

The abolitionists uncovered evidence in Havana, Cuba, to support the Africans' testimony that their status papers were forged. Even though the judge ordered that the Africans could return to Africa, President Van Buren ordered the case be brought before the U.S. Supreme Court. The abolitionists asked former President John Quincy Adams to represent the Africans.

Adams' argument before the Supreme Court lasted two days. He argued, among other things, that the president should not give in to the Spanish demands for the return of the prisoners because it would violate the Constitution by interfering with the judicial system. It also violated the "rights of the negroes, of the citizens, and of the States."[9]

In the end, the Africans prevailed and returned to their country in 1842. The case became a moral victory for abolitionists, but did little to end slavery in America.

A RADICAL ANSWERS THE CALL TO VIOLENCE

HENRY HIGHLAND GARNET WAS NOT A REBEL leader. He did not lead fugitive slaves into revolt, but he led with words—words that advocated that slaves should take up arms and free themselves. But historian Martin Pasterniak calls him "the most influential black American of the nineteenth century."[1] He was one of the first black militants to advocate mass slave uprisings in a public forum when most black and white abolitionists were still preaching a nonviolent message.

David Walker's "Appeal"

Before Garnet, in 1829, David Walker, the son of a free black mother and a slave father, wrote a text urging slaves to rebel. He sewed his *Appeal* in the linings of clothing bought by black sailors. He did this because he knew that black sailors were free to move among different groups and

Henry Highland Garnet advocated for slaves to rise up in violence against their owners.

they could circulate his appeal wherever they landed. Walker hoped his writing would make more abolitionists into militants.[2] But it was Garnet who stood up publicly in 1843 and urged slaves to revolt. And it was John Brown, a white man and abolitionist, who not only supported Garnet's stand, but also put Garnet's words into action.

A White Rebel

John Brown is an exception as the rebel leader. He was neither a slave nor an African American. He was a radical militant and believed in violence to end the institution of slavery. He helped finance the publication of Garnet's speech and David Walker's *Appeal*; both of which urged slaves to resist.[3]

All his life, John Brown was aware of the injustices of slavery. He was born on May 9, 1800, either in Connecticut or as he believed, in New York State. But he was raised in Ohio. His father, a religious man, was openly hostile to

African-American seamen helped deliver messages, including David Walker's *Appeal*, to slaves on Southern plantations.

Let no man of us budge one step, and let slave-holders come to beat us from our country. America is more our country, than it is the whites-we have enriched it with our blood and tears. The greatest riches in all America have arisen from our blood and tears: — and will they drive us from our property and homes, which we have earned with our blood? They must look sharp or this very thing will bring swift destruction upon them. The Americans have got so fat on our blood and groans, that they have almost forgotten the God of armies.[4]

In his *Appeal,* David Walker argues that slaves had earned the right to be Americans because the United States had benefited so greatly from their labor.

those who owned slaves. And John Brown grew up immersed in deeply held abolitionist's beliefs and rigid religious views.[5]

In 1835 as an adult, Brown moved his family to Hudson, Ohio, a center of abolitionist activity. Brown became a stationmaster on the Underground Railroad—a secret network of escape routes to help slaves reach freedom.

The turning point in his life came when an abolitionist publisher, Elijah Lovejoy, was shot to death in Illinois by a proslavery mob. So enraged by this death, John Brown vowed publicly to, "consecrate my life to the destruction of slavery."[6]

As business ventures he had started failed, his abolitionist's beliefs grew more radical. He believed that God was directing him to help end slavery.

John Brown and Bleeding Kansas

Congress passed the Kansas-Nebraska Act in 1854. This act left it up to settlers in these frontier regions to decide how these territories should come into the Union, free or slave. Nebraska stayed mostly antislavery, but hundreds of proslavery and antislavery people moved to Kansas in order to swing the vote their way. Fights, brawls, and battles broke out between the two factions. Soon, Brown joined the fight.

Brown went to Kansas with as many guns and ammunition as he could gather in order to help the antislavery cause. He wound up leading a group of "freestaters" or "Free-Soilers" on guerrilla raids against proslavery camps. One of his raids resulted in the killing of a dozen men and the burning of a Kansas village.[7] President Buchanan offered a $250 reward for John Brown's capture. Brown responded by offering $2.50 for the arrest of Buchanan.[8]

Brown's Last Stand at Harpers Ferry

John Brown dreamed of setting up a fugitive slave colony in the mountains of Virginia and Maryland that would serve as a base for runaway slaves. He believed that from this colony, he could wage war against neighboring slaveholders. By

This picture of John Brown was taken in 1850. Later, he would grow a beard.

continuing to attack and harass them, he would eventually weaken them and therefore weaken the institution of slavery, he thought. This idea led him to attack the United States arsenal at Harpers Ferry, Virginia, on October 16, 1859.

Brown had twenty-one men with him including three of his sons, some slaves, some free men, and some college students.[9] His original plan was to obtain the one hundred thousand weapons at the arsenal and then use the Blue Ridge Mountains as his hideout from which to launch attacks on slave owners.

The night of October 16, Brown and his men crept into the arsenal and overpowered the only guard there. A baggage master from a passing train saw the attack and tried to warn the passengers only to be shot and killed by Brown's men. The Virginia militia was called out and soon eight of Brown's men lay dead, two escaped, and five others were cut off. Those who were left were barricaded with Brown in a fire engine house. An army from Washington, D.C., surrounded them and stormed the engine house, capturing a wounded Brown and the survivors.[10]

A Martyr for the Abolitionist Movement

Brown's trial lasted one week. The jury deliberated for forty-five minutes and found him guilty. Excerpts from his last speech at the trial show that he continued to believe his cause was a just one and that he was following God's laws:

> Now, if it is deemed necessary that I should forfeit my life for the furtherance of the ends of justice, and mingle my blood further with the blood of my children and with the blood of millions in this slave country whose rights are disregarded by wicked, cruel, and unjust enactments—I submit; so let it be done![11]

At age fifty-nine, John Brown was hanged. In the North where abolitionists were many, Brown's death was solemnly observed while the South was jubilant.[12] His last prophecy was that slavery would never be abolished unless through bloodshed. Two years later the Civil War began.

Uprisings Tighten Slavery's Noose

If the goal of each uprising was to free the slaves and abolish slavery, no single rebellion succeeded. And for each insurrection or rumor of insurrection, there was a backlash that resulted in stricter slave laws, harsher punishments, and increased patrols. Of course rebelling was not the only choice; a slave could run away.

TRUANTS, MAROONS, AND RUNAWAYS

MOST SLAVES NEVER JOINED A REBELLION OR used force to gain their freedom. They just left. Some left for a few days, weeks, or months. This was called absenteeism or truancy.[1] Slaves who left for a short period of time may have gone to visit loved ones on a neighboring plantation, may have gone into town, or may have gone as protest against ill treatment.[2] This was another form of resistance.

Life as a Maroon

Those who left for longer periods or stayed in the region might have joined bands of maroons—groups of slaves who lived in the backwoods, hill country, or swamp.[3] These groups were considered outlaws by the plantation owners because they would sometimes steal provisions, sabotage machinery, or persuade other slaves to join them.

Many runaway slaves hid in the woods or swamps.

These maroons developed their own independent settlements where they would raise families. Some of these maroon communities were well organized and exchanged goods, performed work, and traded information with outsiders.[4] Once their transactions were finished, the maroons would disappear back to the swamp or woodlands. When these bands of maroons became a threat to the plantations, they were tracked down and their settlements, if they were found, were destroyed.

Various states had their maroon gangs.[5] Louisiana had such a maroon colony headed by a man named Saint Malo, whose group was periodically tracked. His trackers, however, would always come back without success.[6]

Prior to 1819, Florida had many maroon colonies

because the Spanish government encouraged slaves in Georgia and South Carolina to run away and defend Florida against its enemies. In exchange, the Spanish governor of Florida gave the slaves their freedom.[7] In the Great Dismal Swamp between North Carolina and Virginia, maroons numbered in the thousands.[8]

Maroon bands stayed close to their original plantation, possibly because they had family and friends there who helped them stay alive. But there were other slaves who left the plantation with the intention of never returning. These were runaways.

SOURCE DOCUMENT

In the dark dens of the dismal swamp
The hunted negro lay;
He saw the fire of the midnight camp,
And heard at times the horses' tramp
And a bloodhound's distant bay.

Where Will-o'-the-Wisps and glow-worms shine
In bulrush and in brake,
Where waving mosses shroud the pine,
And the cedar grows, and the poisonous vine
Is spotted like the snake.[9]

This excerpt is from a poem entitled "The Persecuted Negro" by Colonel William Mallory, an ex-slave who served in the Civil War. The poem appeared in Mallory's memoir *Old Plantation Days*.

Runaways Throughout the Centuries

Since 1526, slaves had been running away. Some ran away to find their relatives who had been sold off.[10] Some simply ran away to freedom.

No one knows exactly how many slaves ran, mainly because there is no actual record of escapes. Fugitive slave Samuel Ringgold Ward wrote in his autobiography that he estimated there were thirty-five thousand to forty thousand African Americans in Canada alone; only three thousand he estimated were actually freeborn, meaning the rest may have been fugitive slaves from America.[11] According to author William J. Switala, Southern politicians estimated that there were one hundred thousand runaways between 1810 and 1850. However, these proslavery politicians wanted to inflate the numbers so that they could make the runaway situation seem worse than it was. They wanted compensation either in the form of money or the return of the escaped slaves.[12]

Historians know that the routes fugitive slaves took crisscrossed the United States. The routes went as far as Florida, where some of these fugitives and descendants of fugitives eventually joined bands of Indians, including the Seminoles.[13] The routes also stretched to Mexico in the Southwest.

Fugitives, especially from slave state Texas, slipped into Mexico and formed border communities with the aid of the Mexican government.[14] So many slaves escaped into Mexico that in 1827, Congress proposed a treaty with the Mexican

Slaves had run away since the very beginning of slavery in America. Depicted here is a runaway in the 1600s.

government for the return of runaways. But instead, the Mexican government granted freedom to all slaves in 1829.

By 1847, Texas planters asked President James Polk to develop a plan to force Mexico to return the slaves. Mexico's response in 1850 was to help Seminole American Indians and Seminole blacks. The Mexican government settled them in military colonies in northeast Mexico in return for military service.[15] Besides the Southwest, another route that runaways took went as far as California.

Reverend Thomas Randolph was one of California's black pioneers who founded Mt. Olivet Church in Marysville, California. But Randolph began life as a slave on a Virginia plantation. His escape to freedom began on a coastal schooner arriving in New Bedford, Massachusetts. Then like some other fugitives, he took a ship around Cape Horn at the southern tip of South America and landed in California to begin a new life.[16]

Life as a Runaway

Owners would advertise in newspapers for their slaves' return, hire bounty hunters to find them, and offer rewards for their capture. George Washington placed an ad in the *Maryland Gazette* in 1761, for the return of four slaves who ran away from his plantation:

> Whoever apprehends the said Negroes, . . . shall have, if taken up in this County, Forty Shillings Reward, beside what the Law allows; and if at any greater Distance, or out of the Colony, a proportionable Recompence paid them, by George Washington.[17]

The Great Dismal Swamp was dreaded by runaway slaves.

When fugitive slaves reached their destination, some of them changed their identity so as not to be caught and returned to the slave states. Some slaves returned to bring their relatives out of slavery. Others even told their stories, hoping that they would sway reluctant whites to the abolitionist cause.

RUNAWAYS TELL THEIR STORIES

F REDERICK DOUGLASS ONCE DESCRIBED SLAVERY in the Deep South as "a life of living death."[1] Born as Frederick Augustus Washington Bailey in 1818 in eastern Maryland, he never really knew his mother, Harriet Bailey. She had to work in the cornfields on the plantation, so his grandmother took care of him.

He did not think of himself as a slave during his younger years. But he learned of a person his grandmother called "Old Master." When his grandmother spoke of this person, she did so in fear.[2]

His father's identity is unknown. But Douglass declared in his *Narrative* that his father was white.[3] His mixed racial ancestry also included American Indian.

The Power of the Written Word

One day as a small boy, Frederick was taken to a plantation nearby and left there to grow up with his other siblings. As a boy, he was "given to" several of the owner's relatives. He was told one day that he would be living in Baltimore, Maryland, and was overjoyed to learn he would be leaving the plantation.

While living in Baltimore, he learned how to read and write. With his own money, he bought a copy of *The Columbian Orator*. This was a collection of speeches and essays dealing with liberty, democracy, and courage. That book and other books, along with living in Baltimore where there were many free blacks, would later give him the idea that one day he could get his freedom.[4]

A Severe Blow to the Douglass Family

There was a death on the plantation where Frederick had lived, and the family's property had to be divided among surviving members. He was a slave and was considered property. He was sent back and forth from the old plantation to Baltimore as the family worked on property disputes. He watched as his own family was split up. His grandmother was even evicted from her home and sent to the woods to die.

Getting Stronger by the Day

At the age of fifteen, Frederick settled on a plantation owned by one of the heirs. He received many beatings, but his spirit was not broken. Because of this, he was sent to live on yet another farm where the owner, Edward Covey, was known for being able to break slaves. Frederick endured one beating after another until one day: "[A]t this moment—from whence came the spirit I don't know—I resolved to fight."[5] He grabbed Covey by the throat. The two fought for two hours until Covey stopped. That day, Frederick realized that: "Men are whipped oftenist who are whipped easiest."[6]

Frederick continued working for Covey for a year and then went to work on another plantation. It was then, at sixteen, that he started a secret school for slaves and also plotted to run away.

He and several boys would meet after school and would plan how they would escape. They decided to steal a boat to help them get to Pennsylvania, a free state. But in 1836, when they were about to run, someone informed on them, and Frederick Douglass was put in jail.

Douglass on the Run

Two years later, Douglass disguised himself as a sailor and, obtaining papers from a free seaman, escaped from slavery. Within a week, he was joined by his fiancée, Anna Murray, a free black woman whom he had met in Baltimore.

Once in New York, the couple received help from abolitionist David Ruggles. The couple was married and moved from New York to New Bedford, Massachusetts, where there was a large free black population. It was there that Frederick Bailey changed his name to Douglass, based on a character from a Sir Walter Scott novel. It was in New Bedford where he chose to work as a skilled tradesman. He also became an abolitionist.

SOURCE DOCUMENT

. . . when we permitted ourselves to survey the road, we were frequently appalled. Upon either side we saw grim death, assuming the most horrid shapes. Now it was starvation, causing us to eat our own flesh;—now we were contending with the waves, and were drowned;—now we were overtaken, and torn to pieces by the fangs of the terrible bloodhound. We were stung by scorpions, chased by wild beasts, bitten by snakes, and finally, after having nearly reached the desired spot,—after swimming rivers, encountering wild beasts, sleeping in the woods, suffering hunger and nakedness,—we were overtaken by our pursuers, and, in our resistance, we were shot dead upon the spot![7]

Frederick Douglass would later write about the fears that many slaves had when contemplating whether or not to escape.

Work in New Bedford was not easy to find. Douglass was forced to work as a common laborer as opposed to the skilled trade of a ship caulker because white shipyard employees did not want to work beside blacks. One day he was asked if he wanted to subscribe to the *Liberator*, an abolitionist newspaper published by the outspoken leader

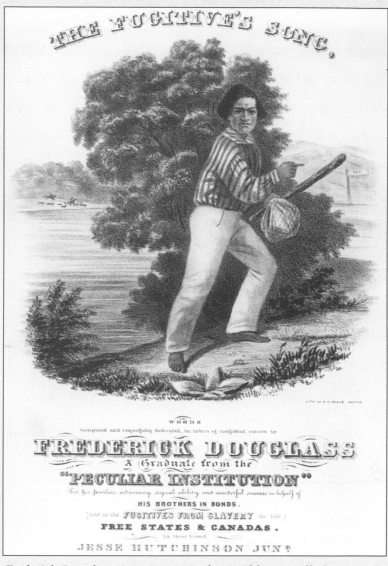

Frederick Douglass was a runaway who would eventually become one of the leading voices for the abolition of slavery. This is the cover of printed sheet music to a song about Douglass's escape from slavery. The printing of sheet music helped people bring popular music of the North into the South.

of the American Anti-Slavery Society, William Lloyd Garrison. "The paper became my meat and drink," wrote Douglass. "My soul was set afire."[8]

Frederick Douglass: The Famous Abolitionist

Douglass became a member of the American Anti-Slavery Society. He became a preacher at the African-American Zion Methodist Church. He spoke out against a popular idea fostered by the American Colonization Society that free blacks should be sent back to Africa. His anti-colonization statements were published by the *Liberator*. Eventually he met Garrison and followed the publisher's philosophy of nonviolence and the idea that moral persuasion would sway people to the antislavery cause. Both Garrison and Douglass also believed in giving women the right to vote.

Douglass traveled for twenty years with other abolitionists and became a powerful speaker. One person who heard Douglass speak wrote that he "was chaste in language, brilliant in thought, truly eloquent in delivery."[9] But some whites doubted that his slave story was true because he was such an eloquent speaker. They did not think that someone so well spoken could have been born a slave.

Douglass decided to write his own story: *Narrative of the Life of Frederick Douglass, an American Slave*. It became an immediate best seller, but it also put him in jeopardy because now everyone knew he was a fugitive. He decided to go to England where slavery was now outlawed.

There he gained an international reputation as a speaker and writer.

He eventually moved back to the United States, settled in Rochester, New York, and published his own abolitionist paper *The North Star*. His views on how to end slavery began to differ from that of his mentor, William Lloyd Garrison. This caused a rift between the two men. Douglass, who had denounced Henry Highland Garnet's speech about the overthrow of slavery through violence, was now advocating a more militant stand.[10]

When John Brown planned to take over the arsenal at Harpers Ferry, he consulted Douglass. Even though Douglass had become more militant in his views, he did not approve of what Brown was going to do because he thought it was not workable.[11]

During the Civil War, Douglass became an advisor to President Abraham Lincoln and was an advocate of enlisting black men as soldiers. Even after the war and the emancipation of slaves, Douglass continued to fight for the rights of African Americans until he died in 1895.

Harriet Tubman

In 1820, Harriet Tubman was born Araminta Ross to parents from the Ashanti tribe in West Africa. Her parents worked on the Brodas plantation in Dorchester County, Maryland.[12] Brodas produced lumber, but also raised slaves to rent and sell. At the age of five, Harriet was hired out to work as a house servant. When she was twelve, she tried to block a doorway to prevent an overseer from punishing a field hand. The overseer picked up an iron weight and threw it, hitting Harriet in the head. From then until old age, she suffered from her injury. She would sometimes blackout.[13]

As a young woman slave in 1844, she married a free African American, John Tubman. She took his last name and later the name of her mother, Harriet. By 1849, Tubman found out that she and other slaves were going to be sold. She had seen two older sisters sold. A story of Tubman's life, written by Sarah H. Bradford in 1886, describes Tubman's fear of being torn from her family:

> Already the inward monitor was whispering to her, "Arise, flee for your life!" and in the visions of the night she saw the horsemen coming, and heard the shrieks of women and children, as they were being torn from each other, and hurried off no one knew whither.[14]

Tubman vowed to run away. According to Bradford, Harriet told her brothers what she was going to do by hinting in a song. She hoped they would follow her when she sang:

> When dat ar ole chariot comes,
> I'm gwine to lebe you,
> I'm boun' for de promised land,
> Frien's, I'm gwine to lebe you.[15]

(Tubman's biographer, a white woman, quoted Tubman as she thought the ex-slave spoke. This does not necessarily mean that Tubman spoke this way.)

No one but her brothers went with her, and even they

Harriet Tubman was an inspiration to many slaves.

turned back eventually. Tubman was left to make the journey alone. With the help of a white neighbor who wrote down the names of two people who could help her, Tubman headed north until she reached Philadelphia.

She described her reaction when she knew she was safely in a free state:

"I looked at my hands," she said, "to see if I was de same person now I was free. Dere was such a glory ober ebery-thing, de sun came like gold trou de trees, and ober de fields, and I felt like I was in heaven."[16]

She worked and saved her money. The next year she decided to return to Maryland to help other slaves escape.

John P. Parker

When John P. Parker was in his fifties in the 1880s, he told about his life as a slave to a journalist who later wrote Parker's autobiography.[17] But the autobiography was not published until 1996.

Most of John Parker's childhood was spent running

away. At eight, he was taken from his mother, bound to an older slave, and forced to walk almost ninety-five miles to Richmond, Virginia. There, he was sold and marched to Mobile, Alabama; a distance of 855 miles.

> Imagine yourself chained to a long chain to which men, women, and children were also attached. The roads were dusty or muddy the June I walked in such a convoy. . . . Ragged and barefooted, I was resentful of the freedom of nature.[18]

He tells of an incident along the way where a bigger slave boy took the food of a smaller slave boy. John was so angry at this that he beat the bigger boy and says that from that day on, "I was the champion of the weak."[19]

When he reached Mobile, he was sold to a doctor whose sons secretly helped John to read. When he was older, he was apprenticed to a harsh tradesman who beat him so badly that he had to go to a hospital for slaves. There, the woman who took care of the ill slaves would also beat them. John witnessed one of these beatings and without thinking, took the whip away from her and beat her with it. A slave striking a white person, let alone a white woman, was a possible death sentence. John knew he had to get away from Mobile before he was caught.

As a runaway, John says he was worth $1,800 and anyone who helped him escape was considered a thief. But he did receive help.

In New Orleans, he stole into a house where a cook gave him food. Then as a stowaway on a boat, he was fed by

Whenever a slave like John P. Parker escaped, the slave catchers were often close behind.

one of the deckhands. But he was caught and forced to work on a farm. He soon escaped, found another boat, was caught, and escaped again, and again stowed away on a boat . . . and again found out.

John always found some way to escape. Finally, after escaping and being recaptured time after time, he found himself back with his old master—the doctor—apprenticed to the owner of an iron foundry.

John became an iron molder, but it did not last because he got into a fight with a supervisor. The doctor who owned him had had enough and was going to apprentice him to an iron foundry in New Orleans. John did not want to go because slaves in New Orleans were often treated even more cruelly than elsewhere. He searched for someone who could buy him. He pleaded with a white woman to pay for him with the promise he would repay the money in two years. She agreed and he became the slave of Mrs. Ryder.

> Each week I not only paid my installment but also frequently doubled it, so at the end of six months I had made a very substantial payment on my contract. Mrs. Ryder was pleased and I was more delighted at the prospect of my early freedom. At the time I was 18, strong as an ox, and working like a steam engine, under high pressure. Another six months would see me in sight of the end of slavery.[20]

He paid his debt. It took him years, but finally he was a free man.

Douglass, Tubman, and Parker were all runaways. At some point in their lives they were either taken away from their families or they saw their relatives sold. They endured harsh punishments and all these experiences advanced their personal fight against the institution of slavery.

THE FUGITIVE SLAVE ACT

SOME RUNAWAYS USED ELABORATE ESCAPE routes that took months, even years, of detailed planning. Some ran at the spur of the moment when they had the opportunity. Most traveled old trails at night and slept during the day, so as not to be caught. Some went alone. Others took family or traveled in groups. But like Douglass, Tubman, and Parker, there were those runaways who were aided in their journey to freedom. Many of the people who helped runaways were doing it out of an individual act of conscience. They may have been abolitionists, free blacks, other slaves, American Indians, and white sympathizers. Individual effort became a loose network called the Underground Railroad. This network became more organized, particularly after 1850 when the Fugitive Slave Act was passed.

Getting Tough on Fugitives

The Fugitive Slave Act came about because as more states joined the Union, the North and South fought over whether these states should come in free or slave. The question came to a head when the United States won the Mexican War in 1846. Because of that war, the United States gained a large tract of land that included California. And when gold was discovered there in 1848, there was pressure to bring California into the union as a free state. This created deeper resentment between Northerners and Southerners.[1]

United States Senator Henry Clay proposed a series of bills. These bills were known as the Compromise of 1850. The antislavery faction gained California as a free state. The proslavery faction gained Texas as a slave state. Among these bills was the Fugitive Slave Act, which reinforced the right of a slave owner to retrieve runaway slaves, even if they were found in a free state. It meant that nowhere in the United States could an African American feel truly safe. Fugitive slaves who lived for years in free states could be arrested and sent back. Free African Americans were even caught and jailed and sent south on the pretext that they were fugitives. And anyone who aided runaway slaves were fined, jailed, and made to pay back the slave owner for the loss of his human property.

Citizens could be deputized against their will to aid in capturing the presumed fugitive slaves.[2] Historians believe this act was responsible for a rebellion that broke out on September 11, 1851, in Christiana, Pennsylvania, when slave

This poster commemorates the Compromise of 1850. At the time, people were optimistic that the set of laws would prevent civil war.

catchers tried to capture several runaways who belonged to Edward Gorsuch.[3] One of the only ways African Americans could feel safe was if they migrated to a country that outlawed slavery.

William Whipper

In one case, the town of Columbia, Pennsylvania, lost its sizeable African-American population because of the Fugitive Slave Act. A wealthy African-American businessman in the town named William Whipper was a partner in a lumber company and many other businesses.[4] He was an active abolitionist as well as an Underground Railroad conductor who sheltered slaves and sometimes helped them escape in his railroad cars that also carried his lumber. He wrote another abolitionist about how the Fugitive Slave Act changed the town in which he lived:

> The colored population of the Borough of Columbia, in 1850, was nine hundred and forty-three, about one-fifth the whole population, and in five years they were reduced to four hundred and eighty-seven by emigration to Canada.[5]

This Compromise of 1850 was voted into law in September of that year and became the turning point of the abolitionist movement because those who had been neutral about slavery now objected to this act. Slave hunters began roaming into free states looking for fugitive slaves and sometimes kidnapping free African Americans. According to Whipper, the people in his town thought they could take

Abolitionists often helped slaves escape to the North.

care of themselves, but then the authorities arrested a citizen. Whipper describes what happened:

> A prominent man, by the name of Baker, was arrested . . . and afterwards purchased by our citizens; another, by the name of Smith was shot dead in one of our lumber yards, because he refused to surrender, and his pursuer permitted to escape without arrest or trial.[6]

After the passage of the Fugitive Slave Act, many whites and blacks vowed to defy the law and join the resistance movement known as the Underground Railroad.

THE UNDERGROUND
RAILROAD

THERE ARE SEVERAL VERSIONS ABOUT HOW THE Underground Railroad got its name. John P. Parker, an Underground Railroad conductor, said in his autobiography that the Underground Railroad originated in Ripley, Ohio. He mentions that shortly after the War of 1812, in a shipyard outside of Ripley, a fugitive ran among piles of lumber and disappeared. The master asked a shipyard workman if he had seen the fugitive. The workman replied, "The slave disappeared too quickly. He must have gone on an underground road."[1] But this is only one version.

All the versions make reference to the frustration slave owners and slave hunters had when hotly pursuing runaways. These pursuers would be close on the heels of fugitives only to find that the fugitives would disappear from sight. They believed the runaways had somehow gone underground on a "road" or by "rail" or "railroad."[2]

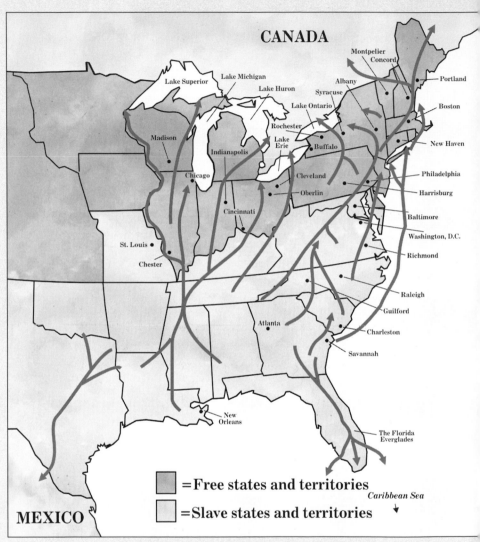

CANADA

Montpelier
Concord

Lake Superior   Lake Michigan   Albany   Portland

Lake Huron   Syracuse

Lake Ontario   Boston

Rochester

Madison   Lake Erie   Buffalo   New Haven

Indianapolis

Chicago   Cleveland   Philadelphia

Oberlin   Harrisburg

Cincinnati   Baltimore

Washington, D.C.

St. Louis   Richmond

Chester

Raleigh

Guilford

Atlanta   Charleston

Savannah

New
Orleans   The Florida
Everglades

= Free states and territories

Caribbean Sea

MEXICO   = Slave states and territories

Most routes on the Underground Railroad led to Canada, where it was illegal for slaves to be sent back to their owners in America.

A Complex Network to Freedom

Regardless of what version of the Underground Railroad's origin is told, the fact is that once some slaves crossed over to free states, slave catchers were unable to find them.

The Underground Railroad was a loosely constructed network of routes that originated in the South. This system used terms similar to a railroad. The Underground Railroad had its "passengers" who were fugitive slaves. The places where they were sheltered were known as "stations" and "depots." "Agents" were people whose homes were used as depots. And those who guided and aided slaves in their escape were called "conductors." "Superintendents" coordinated the Underground Railroad for a state.[3] Historian William J. Switala describes a runaway's arrival to a depot:

> When a traveler arrived at a depot or station house, the usual procedure was to signal his or her arrival by a tap on the door or a window after sundown. The runaway would then be admitted into a darkened room. The windows were covered, the lights turned up, and food and shelter were provided.[4]

"Follow the Drinking Gourd"

There were code names and passwords. There were signs and signals. A quilt with a particular pattern hung on a clothes line to show slaves the direction of a safe house or where to run. A song could also give slaves information about when to run and where to run:

> *When the sun comes back and the first quail calls,*
> *Follow the Drinking Gourd.*

SOURCE DOCUMENT

. . . a white man would carry a certain number of slaves for a certain amount, and if they did not all have money, then those that had had to raise the sum that was required . . . one of us would go to the slaves and find out how many wanted to go, and then we would inform the party who was to take them, and some favorable night they would meet us out in the woods; we would then blow a whistle, and the man in waiting would answer "all right;" he would then take his load and travel by night, until he got into a free State. . . . At one time the kidnappers were within one mile of me; I turned the corner of a house, and went into some bushes, and that was the last they saw of me. The way we abolitionists had of doing our business was called the underground railroad; . . . [5]

James Williams was a fugitive slave who became a conducter on the Underground Railroad and an abolitionist. In his memoirs, he described how the railroad worked.

*For the old man is waiting for to carry you to freedom,
If you follow the Drinking Gourd.*[6]

"Drinking gourd" refers to the Big Dipper star constellation. A person can follow a line from the two stars at the end of the Big Dipper to the North Star, which will guide a person north.

Lights in a window pronounced that it was a safe house. These measures were necessary because anyone aiding, guiding, or sheltering a fugitive slave was at risk of being jailed or put in financial or physical harm.

Those Who Helped Others

A free African American and staunch abolitionist, William Still became a member of the Philadelphia Vigilance Committee, which helped fugitives. He also was Chairman of the Pennsylvania Abolition Society. In these roles he interviewed the newly arrived slaves. He wrote his interviews down and hid his notes. Years later in 1873, he turned his notes into a book. In his book, William Still talks about the arriving runaways:

> Occasionally fugitives came in boxes and chests, and not infrequently some were secreted in steamers and vessels, and in some instances journeyed hundreds of miles in skiffs [rafts or small boats]. Men disguised in female attire and women dressed in the garb of men have under trying circumstances triumphed in thus making their way to freedom.[7]

The people who helped runaways came from all walks

of life. They were farmers, doctors, and ministers. They were often abolitionists—people who worked actively to end slavery by contributing money, petitioning, preaching, politicking, or writing.

Some of these people were enslaved as crew members aboard ships, railroads, and ferries. They hid slaves among the cargo and luggage. They were field workers who could hide a fugitive among the slave population. They were also freemen who risked their own freedom to help slaves. They were whites as well as blacks. They were all people who had something to lose by helping another person run to freedom.

Some Underground Railroad participants were deeply religious and slavery went against their religious beliefs. The Quakers and Mennonites were among this group. As early as 1693, a Quaker printed a pamphlet that argued against slavery. In 1754, the Quakers publicly denounced slavery in all its forms.[8]

Levi Coffin was a Quaker and famous Underground Railroad conductor in Ohio and Indiana. He said that he personally helped thousands of slaves reach freedom in a twenty-year period. When asked why he did it, Coffin said:

> I read in the Bible when I was a boy that it was right to take in the stranger and administer to those in distress, and that I thought it was always safe to do right. The Bible, in bidding us to feed the hungry and clothe the naked, said nothing about color, and I should try to follow out the teachings of that good book.[9]

Women were also part of the Underground Railroad.

Levi Coffin's home in 1837

They not only raised money for the cause and provided clothes and food for newly arriving fugitives, but some acted as conductors or stationmasters.

Sojourner Truth and Harriet Tubman had been slaves. Truth talked publicly across the country about the evils of slavery, while Tubman risked her life to rescue fellow slaves from bondage. Frederick Douglass, a former slave, was a Rochester, New York, Underground Railroad stationmaster. John P. Parker would sneak into Kentucky and bring fugitive slaves back to Ohio where they would be relayed from one depot to another until they were safely out of harm's way.

Every story about the Underground Railroad tells of deeds by ordinary American people. These ordinary citizens formed the Underground Railroad, and desperate slaves hoping to be free were their passengers.

PASSENGERS ON THE UNDERGROUND

HENRY BROWN WRITES IN HIS AUTOBIOGRAPHY that his early childhood was relatively comfortable. But he was prompted to seek freedom in the North when his wife and child were taken away from him.[1]

Henry Brown's Life as a Slave

Henry Brown was born in Louisa County, Virginia, in 1815. He and his family had shoes and clothes to wear, food to eat, and were not treated harshly.

When Brown's owner died, the man's property was divided among the heirs. Brown's family was separated. Brown and his mother and one sister went to live with one son, William Barrett. His other siblings went to live with another son.

Brown was again separated from his family when he went to work in Richmond, Virginia, leaving his remaining family on the William Barrett plantation.

Brown grew up and married a slave girl named Nancy. But before he married her, he appealed to his owner as well as hers asking that they never be sold away from each other. Both men agreed.

However, one day Samuel Cottrell came to him and told him that his wife's owner was going to sell her. Cottrell wanted to buy her, but was shy fifty dollars. Brown loaned the man the fifty dollars, hoping that in this way he would be able to stay with his wife. But when Cottrell bought Nancy, he also threatened to sell her. Brown paid him not to sell her. But Cottrell continued to extort money and favors from Brown. Finally, one day Cottrell asked for more money than Brown had.

Before the end of the day, Brown learned that his wife and children had been sold. He had been married for twelve years and even though he appealed to everyone to advance him money to buy his wife and children, no one would. Brown watched while they marched by in chains. He later wrote:

> Thus passed my child from my presence—it was my own child—I loved it with all the fondness of a father; but things were so ordered that I could only say, farewell, and leave it to pass in its chains while I looked for the approach of another gang in which my wife was also loaded with chains. My eye soon caught her precious face, but, gracious heavens! that glance of agony may God spare me from ever again enduring![2]

The Man in the Box

With everyone he loved gone, Brown decided to run away. He found a shopkeeper he could trust and asked him to help. The shopkeeper told him of plans that others had used as an escape, but those plans did not suit Brown. Brown prayed and an inspiration came to him; he would shut himself in a box. Brown was able to have a box built big enough for him to fit into it. He faked an injury so he would not be missed at work. He had the storekeeper write to a friend in Philadelphia asking permission for the box to be sent there.

The day came when the shopkeeper and another friend nailed Brown inside the box with a bag that held water and some biscuits. They had made three small holes so he could breathe and wrote on the top of the box: "This Side Up With Care." He was on his way to Philadelphia, a distance of 350 miles. It took twenty-seven hours and much of that Brown spent upside down, despite the sign.

He wound up in the Philadelphia office of the Anti-Slavery Society where Brown could hear a number of people talking. In that room was William Still, member of the Vigilance Committee of Philadelphia, who gave this eyewitness account:

> The door had been safely locked. . . . Mr. McKim rapped quietly on the lid of the box and called out, "All right!" Instantly came the answer from within, "All right, sir!" . . . Saw and hatchet quickly had the five hickory hoops cut and the lid off, and the marvelous resurrection of Brown

Henry "Box" Brown was greeted by a number of relieved abolitionists upon his arrival in Philadelphia.

ensued. Rising up in his box, he reached out his hand, saying, "How do you do, gentlemen?"[3]

Brown even composed a song about his exploits. Here is one of the six verses.

When they got to Philadelphia they said he was in port,
And Brown then began to feel glad,
He was taken on the waggon to his final destination,
And left, "this side up with care."[4]

The Crafty Crafts

Another celebrated runaway escape took place in 1848, by a couple who posed as an owner and a slave, William and Ellen Craft. William gave this reason for running away:

. . . we felt perfectly justified in undertaking the dangerous and exciting task of "running a thousand miles" in order to obtain those rights which are so vividly set forth in the Declaration.[5]

Ellen Smith Craft was born in 1826 in the town of Clinton, Georgia, to a slave mother and a prominent citizen of Macon, Georgia, who owned Ellen's mother. Ellen was so fair in complexion that people who visited the plantation would mistake the slave owner's wife as her birth mother. This angered the woman so much that eleven-year-old Ellen was given away as a wedding present to her own half-sister. Ellen was separated from her mother and her childhood friends. She then moved to Macon, Georgia, where she met her future husband, William.

William was the slave of Ira Taylor. William writes that his master sold his mother and father to different persons, "to be dragged off never to behold each other again, till summoned to appear before the great tribunal of heaven."[6] William was also separated from a brother and sister the same way. His master apprenticed William to learn a trade as a cabinetmaker. But then, William writes, his master needed money, so he sold William's brother and mortgaged William and a sister to a bank.

His master could not pay the bank bill when the loan came due, so William and his sister were later sold at auction. His sister was sold first and William watched her go.

This seemed more than I could bear. It appeared to swell my aching heart to its utmost. But before I could fairly recover, the poor girl was gone;—gone, and I have never had the good fortune to see her from that day to this![7]

William had known Ellen for several years before they got married. Ellen did not want to have children because she and her husband had experienced how children were taken away from slave parents. Instead, they thought of a way that they could live as a married couple and have a family, but this meant that they had to run away.

A Complicated Plan

The plan seemed easy, but executing it would be the most difficult adventure they ever undertook. The plan was for Ellen to dress up as a white male slave owner who was being accompanied by his slave. This meant that they would be out in public for the duration of the time they had to travel. There were two very big problems. Even though

Ellen and William Craft executed an escape plan that required intelligence and bravery.

Ellen was extremely fair and could pass for white, she had no facial hair. But by wearing a bandage around her chin, as if she had been in an accident, they were able to disguise that fact. This relieved her of holding long conversations. Glasses covered her face. But there was an added problem, neither Ellen nor William could read or write and they knew that Ellen would have to sign her name eventually. So, they put Ellen's arm in a sling, which prevented her from using her writing hand.

Danger at Every Corner

William sneaked around town to get the necessary disguises. On the day they planned to escape, William went to the train first and got in the "negro" car while Ellen bought two tickets and boarded. But they were not out of danger yet because they saw a man that William worked with. William thought the man would recognize them.

> Fully believing that we were caught, I shrank into a corner, turned my face from the door, and expected in a moment to be dragged out. The cabinet-maker looked into my master's [Ellen's] carriage, but did not know him in his new attire, and as God would have it, before he reached mine the bell rang, and the train moved off.[8]

They first had to travel to Savannah by train and all through that train ride Ellen sat next to someone who knew her master. Ellen pretended to be deaf so she would not have to talk. From Savannah, they took an omnibus (large hired vehicle) to Charleston, South Carolina.

From Charleston, they had to travel by steamer or train through a number of cities. At each place, people inquired about the "invalid's" health and warned about taking a slave north for fear the slave would run away. To each inquiry, Ellen never broke her disguise. But in Baltimore, Ellen and William were summoned to an office. Ellen, as the master, had to tell the authorities why she was taking a slave to a free state. William describes what Ellen said.

SOURCE DOCUMENT

. . . "It is against our rules, sir, to allow any person to take a slave out of Baltimore into Philadelphia, unless he can satisfy us that he has a right to take him along." "Why is that?" asked my master," with more firmness than could be expected. "Because, sir," continued he, in a voice and manner that almost chilled our blood, "if we should suffer any gentleman to take a slave past here into Philadelphia; and should the gentleman with whom the slave might be travelling turn out not to be his rightful owner; and should the proper master come and prove that his slave escaped on our road, we shall have him to pay for;"[9]

William Craft describes a close call while trying to escape from slavery. The "master" he refers to is actually his wife, Ellen, who was posing as a crippled slave owner.

"I bought tickets in Charleston to pass us through to Philadelphia, and therefore you have no right to detain us here." "Well, sir," said the man indignantly, "right or no right, we shan't let you go." Those sharp words fell upon our anxious hearts like the crack of doom, and made us feel that hope only smiles to deceive.[10]

The fugitive couple and officer stared at each other until the silence was broken by the train whistle, announcing the train's departure. The officer backed down and let them board. They were on their way to freedom.

A steamship was one of the modes of transportation that runaway slaves William and Ellen Craft used to escape to the North.

Free in Philadelphia

Finally, they reached Philadelphia—eight days; four trains, one omnibus, and three steamers later—a thousand miles from where they started in Macon, Georgia. And who was among the people to greet them but William Still, the African-American abolitionist who had also greeted Henry "Box" Brown. Still wrote:

> Never can the writer forget the impression made by their arrival. Even now, after a lapse of nearly a quarter of a century, it is easy to picture them in a private room, surrounded by a few friends—Ellen in her fine suit of black, with her cloak and high heeled boots, looking in every respect, like a young gentleman; . . . [11]

Ellen became ill from the ordeal, but she soon recovered and the couple went on to live in Boston where they were married before the law. They publicly spoke about their exploits until they were chased by slave catchers. They decided to leave America and go to England soon after the Fugitive Slave Act of 1850 was passed, because they were no longer safe—even in a free state. They spent many years in England, had five children, and received an education. After the Civil War, the family moved to Savannah to start a farm and a school for ex-slaves. But the Ku Klux Klan burned the first school down and the second school's reputation was ruined by gossip and rumor.[12] Ellen died in 1891 and William died a few years later.

Not all runaways made it to the North themselves. Some were helped along by the daring conductors of the Underground Railroad.

CONDUCTORS ON THE UNDERGROUND

J OHN P. PARKER, EVEN IN HIS OLD AGE, LONG after slavery, always walked in the middle of the street as opposed to walking on the sidewalk. He said he got into the habit of walking in the middle of the street because, as an Underground Railroad conductor in Ripley, Ohio, he had a price on his head. There was always a chance that someone hiding in Ripley's narrow alleys could ambush him on the sidewalk. Parker told his autobiographer that, as an Underground Railroad conductor, he had helped over four hundred slaves to freedom in the North or in Canada.[1]

Help in Ohio

When John Parker came to Ripley, Ohio as a free man, he came to a town that was hotly divided between proslavery and antislavery forces. Ripley, Ohio, was one of the places where both groups could act on their beliefs.

Ripley is located on one side of the Ohio River and Kentucky is located on the other side. Kentucky was a slave state while Ohio was a free state. A slave in Kentucky could look across the river to freedom, and have it if he was able to cross. John Parker, along with other abolitionists in the town like Reverend John Rankin, made it possible for slaves to get across. But since Ripley was an obvious place where slaves could run, it was also where bounty hunters and slave catchers roamed the streets looking for fugitives. According to Parker:

> The woods were patrolled nightly by constables, and any man black or white had to give a good account of himself, especially if he were a stranger. Every ford was watched, while along the creeks and the river, the skiffs were not only pulled up on shore, but were padlocked to trees, and the oars removed. There were dogs in every dooryard, ready to run down the unfortunates.[2]

Parker guided slaves out of Kentucky. By day he worked at his trade as an iron molder, but by night, he became one of the courageous conductors who risked his life to help slaves escape.

He either went across the river to guide slaves out or he helped shelter, feed, and clothe slaves after they crossed. He told of one incident where a man and his wife were determined to cross, but there was no boat. The man put his wife on a log and he got in the water on the Kentucky side and kicked across. They arrived at Parker's house at midnight, dripping wet and exhausted. "Before morning I had fed them, dried them, and taken them over the hill to a place of safety."[3]

Parker, along with some others who helped slaves, lived in houses along the Ohio riverbank. These houses, he says, were constantly watched by authorities because they were the most likely places where fugitives would be sheltered. And Parker described how the owners were constantly in danger:

> This was a period when men went armed with pistol and knife and used them on the least provocation . . . These were the days of passion and battle which turned father against son, and neighbor against neighbor.[4]

The Light in Rankin's Window

One ally of Parker's was Reverend John Rankin whose home sat on the highest hill in Ripley. Rankin had been driven out of Kentucky by pro-slavers.

At night Rankin or one of his six sons would put a light in their window—a light that could be seen for miles. And it was this light shining in the night that would guide runaway slaves.

Clever Coffin and His Schemes

Parker was also well acquainted with other Underground Railroad workers in his area. He knew and worked with Levi Coffin who ran the Underground Railroad in Cincinnati for a number of years. Coffin invented elaborate schemes to get his fugitives out of harm's way. Sometimes he would hide them in false bottom wagons. Parker said one time Coffin had so many fugitives to convey that he hired a horse-drawn hearse and several carriages, then dressed the fugitives as mourners.[5] One slave woman Coffin aided was said to be the model for Eliza in Harriet Beecher Stowe's *Uncle Tom's Cabin.*

Parker Puts His Life on the Line

But Parker's exploits were just as dramatic. His most exciting adventure was helping a Kentucky slave couple and their baby get across the river to safety. This one exploit almost got him killed.

SOURCE DOCUMENT

In the winter of 1826–27, fugitives began to come to our house, and as it became more widely known on different routes that the slaves fleeing from bondage would find a welcome and shelter at our house, and be forwarded safely on their journey, the number increased. Friends in the neighborhood, who had formerly stood aloof from the work, fearful of the penalty of the law, were encouraged to engage in it when they saw the fearless manner in which I acted, and the success that attended my efforts. . . .[6]

Levi Coffin helped thousands of fugitives on the Underground Railroad. In *Reminiscences of Levi Coffin,* he describes how he got started helping slaves in Indiana and how he influenced others.

Parker had received word that a Kentucky couple wanted to cross over the river, but when he reached the spot where he was supposed to meet them, they were not there. He followed the road to the owner's house where he saw a light burning in the window. He found the slave quarters and the couple. The man told Parker that the owner had found out about the plan. So, to prevent the couple from escaping, the owner was keeping their baby beside his bed. The owner knew that the couple would not try to flee without their child. The owner of the plantation even had a shotgun in his bedroom. If anyone tried to snatch the baby, he would shoot him or her.

The slave woman would not leave her child, and the man was too afraid to rescue it. So Parker had to do it. The woman described what the inside of the house looked like, and while the couple made their way down to the boat, Parker snuck in and made his way to the owner's bedroom.

> Peeping around the foot of the bed, I saw a bundle lying close to the edge. Without waiting to see what it was, I dragged it toward me, and getting a firm hold pulled it off the bed. As I did there was a creak of the [bed] springs and the next moment the room was in darkness.[7]

Parker grabbed the bundle, ran out of the room, out of the house, and down the road with the baby in his arms to meet the couple.

> . . . I heard the crack of a pistol and a bullet went singing over my head. [. . .] seeing the two were about to desert me. I yelled as I went by them I had the baby, and if they

wanted it, they would have to follow me. In a few minutes I heard the patter of their feet on the hard road as they came running after me.[8]

Parker rowed them ashore to the opposite side, but they were still being pursued. He knew if anyone recognized him, he would be caught, his possessions confiscated, and he might be jailed or worse—since he was an African American. He dropped the couple off at another home, ran back to his house, undressed, and jumped into bed. The authorities did come to question him, but he was in his nightclothes and denied knowing anything. He even let them search his house. They could find nothing that would link Parker to the fugitive couple and child.

Back Into the Lion's Den

Even though Harriet Tubman was safely in the North, she returned not once, but nineteen times to the South and conducted between three hundred and four hundred other slaves to freedom, according to her biographer, Sarah Bradford. Philanthropist Franklin B. Sanborn once said that Tubman was, "too *real* a person, not to be true."[9]

Harriet Tubman became a conductor the same year that the Fugitive Slave Act was passed—in 1850.[10] She soon returned to the South to help part of her family escape to Pennsylvania. The second time she returned, she was helped by Quaker and Underground Railroad stationmaster Thomas Garrett, whose home was the last stop on the Underground Railroad leading from slave state Maryland to

Harriet Tubman (left) poses with some of the slaves she saved.

Pennsylvania, a free state. Garrett helped Tubman get one of her brothers and his friends to safety and is said to have helped twenty-seven hundred fugitives.[11]

Tubman made eleven trips to Maryland from 1852–1857. Maryland posted a twelve thousand dollar reward for her capture.[12] Although she went back for her husband, he refused to go with her because he had remarried.

Tubman believed that God guided her. She always was able to find money for her trips, escape detection, and deliver her passengers safely. Garrett believed that she did have some divine force aiding her:

> . . . she called on me again, and said that God told her I had some money for her, but not so much as before.

I had, a few days previous, received the net proceeds of
one pound ten shillings from Europe for her. . . . certain
it was she had a guide within herself other than the written word, for she never had any education.[13]

Wanted: Harriet Tubman

By the mid 1850s the reward for Tubman had grown to as
high as forty thousand dollars, but she continued to make
her trips to the same area from which she herself had
escaped. Sarah Bradford writes about one incident where
Tubman fooled the watchful authorities:

> Suddenly on turning a corner, she spied her old master
> coming towards her. She pulled the string which tied the
> legs of the chickens; they began to flutter and scream,
> and as her master passed, she was stooping and busily
> engaged in attending to the fluttering fowls. And he went
> on his way, little thinking that he was brushing the very
> garments of the woman who had dared to steal herself,
> and others of his belongings.[14]

If Tubman guided women with babies, she would carry
a drug to help keep the babies quiet. She carried a revolver
and threatened to shoot those who wanted to give up. She
once told Frederick Douglass that not once had she ever
lost a passenger.

Her most triumphant rescue was when she was able to
get her parents out. By then, both parents were elderly.
Tubman's father had been arrested and charged for aiding
fugitives. Her father was scheduled to appear in court, but

was not held in custody when Tubman snuck back into Maryland and, according to Garrett:

> They started with an old horse, fitted out in primitive style with a *straw collar*, a pair of old chaise wheels, with a board on the axle to sit on, another board swung with ropes, fastened to the axle, to rest their feet on. She got her parents, who were both slaves belonging to different masters, on this rude vehicle to the railroad, put them in the cars, turned Jehu [*King of Israel known for his rapid chariot driving*] herself, and drove to town in a style that no human being ever did before or since; but she was happy at having arrived safe.[15]

William Still knew Tubman and helped her. Thomas Garrett respected her. She was admired by John Brown, who consulted her before making his ill-fated assault on Harpers Ferry. Frederick Douglass once wrote to Tubman: "Excepting John Brown—of sacred memory—I know of no one who has willingly encountered more perils and hardships to serve our enslaved people than you have."[16]

During the Civil War, she became a spy, nurse, and soldier. Afterwards, she lived out the rest of her days in Auburn, New York until she died in 1913.

However, her legacy lives on, as well as that of other runaways, those who helped them, and slaves who fought for freedom.

SEPARATING TRUTH FROM MYTH

WHAT WAS REAL AND WHAT WAS RUMOR IS difficult to determine when investigating American slave revolts. The rebellions mentioned in this book were widely reported and confirmed in their day through court documents, letters, and diaries or mentioned in newspapers and because of this, they were widely researched. There were, however, many unsupported rumors of slave rebellions, particularly during the 1840s and 1850s in the South.[1] In 1856, it was reported in the newspapers that slaves who were ironworkers in Tennessee were rising up and crossing into Kentucky to revolt. Historian Charles Dew believes this "rebellion" was fueled by white hysteria that eventually resulted in blacks being brutally tortured and killed.[2]

Rebellions During the Civil War

In 1865, there was a rumor that freedmen and slaves were plotting to revolt and seize land and property as revenge against slavery even though slaves would be emancipated anyway at the end of the Civil War and by most accounts, freemen would have nothing to gain by a rebellion.[3] This rumor proved to be unfounded.

But in 1861, at the beginning of the Civil War, there actually was an insurrection in Mississippi near Natchez. According to Historian Winthrop Jordan, three dozen blacks were killed and no whites.[4] But nothing was reported in the paper. There was a conspiracy of silence among the whites in that area. Jordan speculates that Southerners suppressed the news of the uprising because they believed it would fuel widespread rebellion among

Runaway slaves were called contrabands by Union soldiers during the Civil War. These African Americans are learning to read at Freedman's Village in Arlington, Virginia.

Southern slaves, panic whites, and weaken the South's position against the North.

Historian Herbert Aptheker notes, it is difficult to unearth the history of slave revolts in America because of "exaggeration, distortion, and censorship."[5] But finding out information about slave revolts did help in creating a more accurate picture of slavery in America. It countered the belief long held by early-twentieth century writers and historians that slaves were calm and content with their situations.

The Rebels' Place in History

Slave rebels became folk heroes, particularly in times of racial trouble. In the 1960s, slave rebels were heralded for their heroics alongside nonviolent advocates like Martin Luther King, Jr. Heroes, according to historian William L. Van Deburg, "mirror the folk soul, promise power to the weak, and inspire revolt against the mighty."[6] Nat Turner, Denmark Vesey, and John Brown are seen as heroes to some, then and now.

Discovering the Underground Railroad

Just as we learn more about slave uprisings and those who led them, we are also learning more about the Underground Railroad and those who participated in it.

For the most part, many of the Underground Railroad stories will never be told. It was dangerous to keep records, and those who participated in underground activities kept silent for fear that they would be caught. Myth and legend have developed around the Underground Railroad activity.

The search for Underground Railroad routes, safe

houses, persons who helped the fugitive slaves, and the identity of the slaves have become a puzzle that local people and organizations have been piecing together for years. With the aid of national legislation, a national repository of information is being created under the direction of the National Park Service. This national repository is called the Underground Railroad Network to Freedom.

The Underground Railroad Network to Freedom

The network has a three-pronged focus: education; technical assistance; and coordination of programs, facilities, and historic sites.

Local people working on their own and aided by historical organizations and libraries are uncovering data, authenticating stories, and exploring and verifying sites. Some of this information will contribute to building the network. "The information that we have collected so far leads us to believe that it [the Underground Railroad] was more complex than historians traditionally described it," according to Diane Miller, the national coordinator of the Underground Railroad Network to Freedom.[7]

Part of what has already been discovered is that generations of families seemed to have devoted their lives to rescuing slaves. At the center of each of these groups of families were one or more antislavery churches.[8] Also important is the extent that African Americans were involved in the Underground Railroad movement. "The role of the African American community [in the

These stairs lead from the Ohio River to the home of Underground Railroad conductor Reverend John Rankin. This structure is called the "Freedom Stairway" because it is likely that slaves used it to get to Rankin's safehouse.

Underground Railroad] has been underestimated," says Diane Miller.[9]

Eventually, all the information that is being collected on the Underground Railroad will create a living museum of sites, programs, and facilities.

Those interested in history will continue to study the people who struggled against slavery. This way, people will understand how important this period was in American history and how it shapes our thinking today.

1526	Slaves brought to what is now South Carolina by Spanish.
1619	Dutch vessel carrying twenty Africans lands in Jamestown, Virginia.
1642	Virginia colony enacts law to find those who harbor or assist runaway slaves.
1680	First slave law in Virginia forbids slaves to carry weapons.
1712	Slave revolt in New York on April 6.
1731	Slave law forbids slaves to walk the streets of New York without master present.
1739	Stono Rebellion in South Carolina.
1777 −1804	Northern states abolish slavery through state constitutions.
1793	Congress passes the Fugitive Slave Act; Canada bans the importation of slaves and forbids slave holders from entering Canada and retrieving fugitive slaves; Invention of the cotton gin.
1800	Gabriel's Conspiracy.
1804	Haiti declares itself independent.
1808	Importation of slaves banned in United States.
1816	American Colonization Society founded.

1820	Missouri Compromise limits the expansion of slavery.
1822	Denmark Vesey Conspiracy in Charleston, S.C.
1831	Nat Turner Rebellion; William Lloyd Garrison prints first issue of anti-slavery newspaper, *The Liberator.*
1838	Underground Railroad is formally organized; Black abolitionist Robert Purvis becomes chairman of the General Vigilance Committee and "president" of the Underground Railroad; Frederick Douglass runs away.
1839	Fifty-three Africans revolt and free themselves on the *Amistad.*
1843	Henry Highland Garnet calls for slave violence.
1845	Frederick Douglass' autobiography *Narrative of the Life of Frederick Douglass* is published.
1848	Henry "Box" Brown escapes to Philadelphia; William and Ellen Craft disguise themselves as master and slave and escape to Philadelphia.
1849	Harriet Tubman makes her famous escape from Maryland.
1850	Fugitive Slave Act.
1859	Harpers Ferry raid by John Brown.
1860	Republican candidate Abraham Lincoln is elected President of the United States.
1861 –1865	The Civil War.
1865	The Thirteenth Amendment frees all the slaves.

INTRODUCTION

1. Herbert Aptheker, "Slave Rebellions in the United States," *Encarta Africana*, n.d., <http://www.africana.com/research/encarta/rebellion.asp> (October 1, 2003).

2. Ibid.

3. Edward Countryman, ed., *How Did American Slavery Begin?* (New York: Bedford/St. Martin's, 1999), p. 3.

4. Ira Berlin, *Generations of Captivity: A History of African American Slaves* (Cambridge, Mass.: The Belknap Press of Harvard University Press, 2003), p. 23.

5. Ibid., p. 34.

6. Ibid., p. 36.

7. *Underground Railroad, Official National Park Handbook* (Washington, D.C.: Div. of Publications, National Park Service, U.S. Dept. of the Interior, 1998), p. 26.

8. William J. Switala, *Underground Railroad in Pennsylvania* (Mechanicsburg, Pa.: Stackpole Books, 2001), p. 5.

9. Ira Berlin, *Many Thousands Gone: The First Two Centuries of Slavery in North America* (Cambridge, Mass.: The Belknap Press of Harvard University Press, 1998), p. 178.

10. W. Jeffery Bolster, "To Feel Like a Man": *Black Seamen in the Northern States, 1800–1860, The Journal of American History*, vole. 76, no. 4, March 1990, pp. 1173-1199.

11. David Waldstreicher, *The Struggle Against Slavery: A History in Documents* (New York: Oxford University Press, 2001), p. 20.

12. Herbert Aptheker, *American Negro Slave Revolts* (New York: International Publishers, 1993), p. 13.

13. Berlin, *Many Thousands Gone*, p. 78.

14. "Transcription of the Declaration of Independence," U.S. National Archives and Records Administration (NARA), n.d., <http://www.archives.gov/national_archives_experience/declaration_transcript.html> (July 24, 2002).

15. Ibid.

16. Ira Berlin, *Generations of Captivity*, p. 112.

17. *Underground Railroad, Official National Park Handbook*, p. 31.

18. James Roberts, *The Narrative of James Roberts, a Soldier Under Gen. Washington in the Revolutionary War, and Under Gen. Jackson at the Battle of New Orleans, in the War of 1812: "a Battle Which Cost Me a Limb, Some Blood, and Almost My Life,"* (Chicago: Published for the Author, 1858), p. 9, Electronic Edition, "Documenting the American South," *University of North Carolina at Chapel Hill Libraries*, 2001, <http://docsouth.unc.edu/neh/roberts/roberts.html> (March 2, 2004).

19. Alonford James Robinson, Jr., "Free Blacks in the United States," *Encarta Africana*, n.d.,<http://www.africana.com/research/encarta/census.asp> (September 13, 2003).

20. "Eli Whitney's Patent for the Cotton Gin," *Teaching with Documents Lesson Plan: NARA Digital Classroom*, n.d., <http://www.archives.gov/digital_classroom/lessons/cotton_gin_patent/cotton_gin_patent.html> (July 24, 2002).

21. "People and Events: The Haitian Revolution," n.d., <http://www.pbs.org/wgbh/aia/part3/3p2990.html> (August 13, 2002).

CHAPTER 1. UPRISINGS

1. Herbert Aptheker, "Slave Rebellions in the United States," *Encarta Africana*, n.d., <http://www.africana.com/research/encarta/rebellion.asp> (October 1, 2003).

2. Herbert Aptheker, *American Negro Slave Revolts* (New York: International Publishers, 1993), p. 3.

3. Eugene D. Genovese, *From Rebellion to Revolution: Afro-American Slave Revolts in the Making of the Modern World* (Baton Rouge: Louisiana State University Press, 1979), pp. 11–12.

4. Graham Russell Hodges, *Root & Branch: African Americans in New York and East Jersey 1613–1863* (Chapel Hill: The University of North Carolina Press, 1999), p. 65.

5. Willie Lee Rose, ed., *A Documentary History of Slavery in North America* (New York, London, Toronto: Oxford University Press, 1976), p. 100.

6. Hodges, p. 67.

7. Nicholas Halasz, *The Rattling Chains: Slave Unrest and Revolt in the Antebellum South* (New York: David McKay Company, Inc., 1966), p. 20.

8. Roy E. Finkenbine, "Stono Rebellion," *African American Encyclopedia* (Tarrytown, N.Y.: Marshall Cavendish, 1993), vol. 6, p. 1524.

9. Rose, p. 103.

10. William Bull, "Report from William Bull re. Stono Rebellion," *PBS Online: Africans in America,* © 1998, 1999, <http://www.pbs.org/wgbh/aia/part1/1h311t.html> (March 2, 2004).

11. Finkenbine, p. 1526.

CHAPTER 2. A SLAVE REBELS

1. Douglas R. Egerton, *Gabriel's Rebellion, The Virginia Slave Conspiracies of 1800 and 1802* (Chapel Hill: The University of North Carolina Press, 1993), p. 21.

2. "Gabriel's Conspiracy," Africans in America, n.d., <http://www.pbs.org/wgbh/aia/part3/3p1576.html> (August 4, 2002).

3. Ira Berlin, *Generations of Captivity: A History of African American Slaves* (Cambridge, Mass.: The Belknap Press of Harvard University Press, 2003), p. 221.

4. "Gabriel's Conspiracy."

5. Gervas Storrs and Joseph Seldon, "Confession of Solomon," *PBS Online: Africans in America,* © 1998, 1999, <http://www.pbs.org/wgbh/aia/part3/3h494t.html> (March 2, 2004).

6. Willie Lee Rose, ed., *A Documentary History of Slavery in North America* (New York: Oxford University Press, 1976), p. 109.

7. Herbert Aptheker, *American Negro Slave Revolts* (New York: International Publishers, 1993), p. 249.

CHAPTER 3. A FREE PERSON REBELS

1. Alonford James Robinson, Jr., "Free Blacks in the United States," *Encarta Africana,* n.d., <http://www.africana.com/research/encarta/census.asp> (September 13, 2002).

2. James Thomas McGowan, "Creation of a Slave Society," Ph.D dissertation, (University of Rochester, 1976), p. 106 in Ira Berlin, *Generations of Captivity: A History of African American Slaves* (Cambridge, Mass.: The Belknap Press of Harvard University Press, 2003), p. 143.

3. *Underground Railroad, Official National Park Handbook* (Washington, D.C.: Div. of Publications, National Park Service, U.S. Dept. of the Interior, 1998), p. 37.

4. Robinson, Jr.

5. "American Colonization Society," *Africans in America,* n.d., <http://www.pbs.org/wgbh/aia/part3/3p1521.html> (December 4, 2002).

6. Alonford James Robinson, Jr., "American Colonization Society," *Encarta Africana,* n.d., <http://www.psfdc.org/subpages/PSFinfo/AmericanColonization.htm> (September 9, 2003).

7. Peter C. Ripley, *Witness for Freedom: African American Voices on Race, Slavery, and Emancipation* (Chapel Hill: The University of North Carolina Press, 1993), p. 34.

8. Robinson, Jr., "Free Blacks in the United States."

9. "Soul of America-Charleston: Historical Context," n.d., <http://www.soulofamerica.com/cityfldr/charleston1.html> (November 12, 2002).

10. "Gale Free Resources: Black History Month—Biography, Denmark Vesey," 1999, <http://www.galegroup.com/free_resources/bhm/bio/vesey_d.htm> (November 14, 2002).

11. Michael P. Johnson, "Denmark Vesey and His Co-Conspirators," *The William and Mary Quarterly,* 2001, <http://www.historycooperative.org/journals/wm/58.4/johnson.html> (October 25, 2003).

12. Ibid.

13. "This Far by Faith," <http://www.pbs.org/thisfarbyfaith/people/denmark_vesey.html > (June 24, 2004).

14. "Gale Free Resources: Black History Month—Biography, Denmark Vesey."

15. *Slave Insurrections, Selected Documents.* An Account of the Late Intended Insurrection Among A portion of the Blacks of this City. Published by the Authority of The Corporation of Charleston, Charleston: Printed by A.E. Miller, 4 Broad-Street. 1822 (Westport, Conn.: Negro Universities Press, 1970), p. 8.

16. Ibid., p. 39.

17. Johnson.

18. "This Far by Faith."

CHAPTER 4. VISIONARY OR MADMAN?

1. Videotape, "A Troublesome Property," Director: Charles Burnett, Producer/Writer Frank Christopher, Co-Producer/Writer/Historian Kenneth S. Greenberg, California Newsreel, 60 minutes, 2002.

2. "Nat Turner's Rebellion," *Africans in America,* n.d., <http://www.pbs.org/wgbh/aia/part3/3p1518.html> (January 6, 2002).

3. Thomas R. Gray, MD, *The Confessions of Nat Turner: Leader of the Late Insurrection in Southampton, Va.* (Baltimore: Published by Thomas R. Gray, 1831), p. 138.

4. Thomas Gray, "The Confessions of Nat Turner," *PBS Online: Africans in America,* © 1998, 1999, <http://www.pbs.org/wgbh/aia/part3/3h500t.html> (March 2, 2004).

5. "Nat Turner's Rebellion."

6. Kenneth S. Greenberg, ed., *The Confessions of Nat Turner and Related Documents* (Boston: Bedford Books of St. Martin's Press, 1996), p. 19.

CHAPTER 5. REBELLION AT SEA

1. Joseph Cinque: Reference, n.d., <http://www.pbs.org/wnet/aaworld/reference/articles/joseph_cinque.html> (January 18, 2003).

2. David Richardson, "Shipboard Revolts, African Authority, and the Atlantic Slave Trade," *The William and Mary Quarterly,* 2001, <http://www.historycooperative.org/journals/wm/58.1/richardson.html > (October 26, 2003).

3. Ibid.

4. Ibid.

5. Ibid.

6. Howard Jones, *Mutiny on the Amistad* (New York: Oxford University Press, 1987), p. 14.

7. "The Amistad Case," Smithsonian's National Portrait Gallery, n.d., <http://www.npg.si.edu/col/amistad/index.htm> (January 18, 2003).

8. Jones, p. 26.

9. Ibid., p. 12.

Chapter 6. A Radical Answers the Call to Violence

1. Martin B. Pasterniak, *Rise Now and Fly to Arms: The Life of Henry Highland Garnet,* Ph.D dissertation, University of Massachusetts (University Microfilm International, 1981), p. viii.

2. Walker's Appeal and Garnet's Address (New York: Arno Press and the New York Times, 1969), p. iii.

3. Stephen Oats, *To Purge This Land with Blood: A Biography of John Brown* (New York: Harper & Row, 1970), p. 61 in Joel Schor, *Henry Highland Garnet: A Voice of Black Radicalism in the 19th Century* (Westport, Connecticut and London, England: Greenwood Press, 1977), p. 60.

4. David Walker, "David Walker's Appeal," *PBS Online: Africans in America,* © 1998, 1999, <http://www.pbs.org/wgbh/aia/part4/4h2931t.html> (March 2, 2004).

5. "People and Events: John Brown," *Africans in America,* n.d., <http://www.pbs.org/wgbh/aia/part4/4p1550.html> (December 21, 2002).

6. "John Brown's Holy War," *The American Experience,* n.d., <http://www.pbs.org/wgbh/amex/brown/filmmore/description.html> (January 4, 2002).

7. Bobbie Alton, "John Brown's Half-Sister Also Stood For Freedom," *Monthly Series by the Kansas State History Society*, August 1998, <http://www.kshs.org/features/feat898.htm> (December 29, 2002).

8. "The Missouri Raid," *The American Experience*, n.d., <http://www.pbs.org/wgbh/amex/brown/peopleevents/pande08.html> (December 29, 2002).

9. "John Brown's Holy War."

10. "John Brown," *Netstate.com: Connecticut*, n.d., <http://www.netstate.com/states/peop/people/ct_jb.htm> (December 29, 2002).

11. *John Brown's Speech to the Court at His Trial*, n.d., <http://www.nationalcenter.org/JohnBrown'sSpeech.html> (December 29, 2002).

12. Merrill D. Peterson, *John Brown* (Charlottesville and London: University of Virginia Press, 2002), pp. 27–28.

CHAPTER 7. TRUANTS, MAROONS, AND RUNAWAYS

1. John Hope Franklin and Loren Schweninger, *Runaway Slaves: Rebels on the Plantation* (Oxford: Oxford University Press, 1999), p. 98.

2. William J. Switala, *Underground Railroad in Pennsylvania* (Mechanicsburg, Pa.: Stackpole Books, 2001), p. 103.

3. Franklin and Schweninger, p. 100.

4. John Tidwell, "The Maroons," *American Legacy*, Winter 2003, p. 46.

5. Franklin and Schweninger, p. 86.

6. Tidwell.

7. Ira Berlin, *Generations of Captivity: A History of African American Slaves* (Cambridge, Mass.: The Belknap Press of Harvard University Press, 2003), p. 46.

8. Tidwell.

9. William Mallory, *Old Plantation Days*, Third Edition, p. 2, Electronic Edition, "Documenting the American South," *University of North Carolina at Chapel Hill Libraries*, 1999, <http://docsouth.unc.edu/mallory/mallory.html> (March 2, 2004).

10. Franklin and Schweninger, p. 52.

11. Samuel Ringold Ward, *Autobiography of a Fugitive Negro: His Anti-Slavery Labours in the United States, Canada & England* (London: John Snow, 1855 reprint Arno Press and the New York Times, p. 154) in Switala, p. 14.

12. Ibid.

13. Tidwell.

14. Aaron Mahr Yanez, National Park Service, historian, personal interview, October 1999 and February 2003.

15. Ronnie C. Tyler, "Fugitive Slaves in Mexico," *The Journal of Negro History*, vole. 57, no. 1, January 1972, pp. 1–12.

16. Guy Washington, regional coordinator, Pacific West Region, Underground Network to Freedom, National Park Service, personal interview, October 1999 and February 2003.

17. "Advertisement for Runaway Slaves," *The Papers of George Washington*, n.d., <http://gwpapers.virginia.edu/slavery/aug1761.html> (September 16, 2002).

CHAPTER 8. RUNAWAYS TELL THEIR STORIES

1. Sandra Thomas, *A Biography of the Life of Frederick Douglass, The Slave Years*, n.d., <http://www.history.rochester.edu/class/douglass/part1.html> (January 21, 2003).

2. Ibid.

3. Frederick Douglass, *Narrative of Frederick Douglass*, edited with an Introduction by David W. Blight (Boston and New York: Bedford's Press/St. Martin's Press), pp. 2–5.

4. Thomas.

5. Frederick Douglass, *Narrative of the Life of Frederick Douglass, an American Slave, Written by Himself* (Boston: Published at the Anti-Slavery Office, No. 25 Cornhill, 1845), p. 71, Electronic edition, "Documenting the American South," *University of North Carolina at Chapel Hill Libraries*, 1999, <http://docsouth.unc.edu/douglass/douglass.html> (February 2, 2003).

6. Thomas.

7. Frederick Douglass, *Narrative of the Life of Frederick Douglass, an American Slave, Written by Himself* (Boston: Published at the Anti-Slavery Office, No. 25 Cornhill, 1845), p. 85, Electronic Edition, "Documenting the American South," *University of North Carolina at Chapel Hill Libraries*, 1999, <http://docsouth.unc.edu/douglass/douglass.html> (March 2, 2004).

8. Sandra Thomas, *A Biography of the Life of Frederick Douglass, From Slave to Abolitionist/Editor*, n.d., <http://www.history.rochester.edu/class/douglass/part2.html> (February 6, 2004).

9. The Liberator, July 8, 1842, in Benjamin Quarles, *Frederick Douglass* (Washington, D.C.: The Associated Publishers, Inc., 1969), p. 27.

10. Sandra Thomas, *A Biography of the Life of Frederick Douglass, The Rochester Years*, n.d., <http://www.history.rochester.edu/class/douglass/part3.html> (February 6, 2003).

11. Ibid.

12. Rachel Shalman, "Spectrum Home and School Network: Harriet Tubman," <http://www.incwell.com/Biographies/Tubman.html> (June 24, 2004).

13. "Harriet Tubman: The Moses of Her People," electronic version, (University of North Carolina at Chapel Hill, 1995), <http://docsouth.unc.edu/harriet/harriet.html> p. 15.

14. Ibid., pp. 25–26.

15. Ibid., p. 28.

16. Ibid., p. 30.

17. John P. Parker, *His Promised Land*, ed. Stuart Seely Sprague (New York: W.W. Norton & Company, 1996), pp. 12–13.

18. Ibid., pp. 26–28.

19. Ibid.

20. Ibid., p. 67.

CHAPTER 9. THE FUGITIVE SLAVE ACT

1. "Opposing Forces," n.d., <http://www.whispersofangels.com/opposing.html> (February 7, 2003).

2. "The Compromise of 1850," *Africans in America*, n.d., <http://www.pbs.org/wgbh/aia/part4/4p2951.html> (January 12, 2003).

3. William J. Switala, *Underground Railroad in Pennsylvania* (Mechanicsburg, Pa.: Stackpole Books, 2001), pp. 25–26.

4. David Zimmerman, "William Whipper in the Black Abolitionist Tradition," *The Underground Railroad in Lancaster County*, n.d., <http://muweb.millersville.edu/~ugrr/resources/columbia/whipper.html> (February 7, 2003).

5. William Still, *The Underground Railroad* (New York: Arno Press and the New York Times, reprint 1968), p. 739.

6. Ibid., p. 736.

CHAPTER 10. THE UNDERGROUND RAILROAD

1. John P. Parker, *His Promised Land*, ed. Stuart Seely Sprague (New York: W.W. Norton & Company, 1996), p. 87.

2. William J. Switala, *Underground Railroad in Pennsylvania* (Mechanicsburg, Pa.: Stackpole Books, 2001), p. 13.

3. Ibid., pp. 17–18.

4. Ibid.

5. James Williams, *Life and Adventures of James Williams, a Fugitive Slave, with a Full Description of the Underground Railroad* (San Francisco: Women's Union Print, 424 Montgomery Street, 1873), p. 12, Electronic Edition, "Documenting the American South," *University of North Carolina at Chapel Hill Libraries*, 2000 <http://

docsouth.unc.edu/neh/williams/williams.html#p14> (March 2, 2004).

6. "Explanation of Follow the Drinking Gourd," *Nasa Quest*, n.d., <http://quest.arc.nasa.gov/ltc/special/mlk/gourd2.html> (February 10, 2004).

7. William Still, *The Underground Railroad* (New York: Arno Press and the New York Times, 1968), p. 1.

8. Switala, p. 6.

9. "Levi Coffin: President of the Underground Railroad," n.d., <http://afgen.com/coffin1.html> (March 2, 2004).

CHAPTER 11. PASSENGERS ON THE UNDERGROUND

1. Henry Box Brown, "Narrative of the Life of Henry Box Brown, Written by himself," electronic version, <http://docsouth.unc.edu/brownbox/brownbox.html> pp. i–ii, (February 6, 2004).

2. Ibid., p. 47.

3. William Still, *The Underground Railroad* (New York: Arno Press and the New York Times, 1968), p. 83.

4. Brown, p. 61.

5. William Craft, *Running A Thousand Miles for Freedom; or The Escape of William and Ellen Craft from Slavery* (New York: Arno Press and the New York Times, 1969), p. iii.

6. Ibid., p. 9.

7. William Craft, *Running a Thousand Miles for Freedom; or, The Escape of William and Ellen Craft from Slavery* (London: William Tweedie, 337, Strand, 1860), p. 12, Electronic Edition, "Documenting the American South," (University of North Carolina at Chapel Hill Libraries, 2001), <http://docsouth.unc.edu/neh/craft/craft.html> (March 2, 2004).

8. William Craft, *Running A Thousand Miles for Freedom; or, The Escape of William and Ellen Craft from Slavery* (New York: Arno Press and the New York Times, 1969), pp. 42–43.

9. William Craft, *Running a Thousand Miles for Freedom; or, The Escape of William and Ellen Craft from Slavery* (London: William Tweedie, 337, Strand, 1860), p. 71, Electronic Edition, "Documenting the American South,"

University of North Carolina at Chapel Hill Libraries, 2001, <http://docsouth.unc.edu/neh/craft/craft.html> (March 2, 2004).

10. Craft, *Running A Thousand Miles for Freedom; or, The Escape of William and Ellen Craft from Slavery* (New York: Arno Press and the New York Times, 1969), p. 72.

11. William Still, *The Underground Railroad* (New York: Arno Press and the New York Times, 1968), p. 739.

12. "Georgia Women of Achievement: 1996 Inductee, Ellen Smith Craft," n.d., <http://www.gawomen.org/honorees/long/crafte_long.htm> (February 22, 2003).

CHAPTER 12. CONDUCTORS ON THE UNDERGROUND

1. John P. Parker, *His Promised Land*, ed. Stuart Seely Sprague (New York: W.W. Norton & Company, 1996), p. 19.

2. Ibid., p. 72.

3. Ibid., p. 73.

4. Ibid., pp. 85–86.

5. Levi Coffin, *Reminiscences of Levi Coffin* (reprinted New York: Arno Press and the New York Times, 1968), pp. 307–310.

6. Levi Coffin, "Levi Coffin's Underground Railroad station," *PBS Online: Africans in America*, © 1998, 1999 <http://www.pbs.org/wgbh/aia/part4/4h2946t.html> (March 2, 2004).

7. Coffin, *Reminiscences of Levi Coffin*, p. 114.

8. Ibid.

9. "Harriet Tubman, The Moses of Her People," electronic version, (University of North Carolina at Chapel Hill, 1995), n.d., <http://docsouth.unc.edu/harriet/harriet.html> p. 5, (January 24, 2003).

10. "Harriet Tubman Timeline," *African American History of Western New York*, n.d., <http://www.math.buffalo.edu/~sww/0history/hwny-tubman.html> (February 10, 2003).

11. "Thomas Garrett," n.d., <http://www.whispersofangels.com/biographies.html> (August 14, 2003).

12. "Harriet Tubman Timeline."

13. "Harriet Tubman, The Moses of Her People," electronic version, p. 87.

14. Ibid., pp. 34–35.

15. Ibid., pp. 87–88.

16. Ibid., p. 135.

CHAPTER 13. SEPARATING TRUTH FROM MYTH

1. Dan T. Carter, "The Anatomy of Fear: The Christmas Day Insurrection Scare of 1865," *The Journal of Southern History*, vole. 42, no. 3, August 1976, pp. 345-364.

2. Charles B. Dew, "Black Ironworkers and the Slave Insurrection Panic of 1856," *The Journal of Southern History*, vol. 41, no. 3, August 1975, pp. 321-338.

3. Carter.

4. Wintrop D. Jordan, *Tumult and Silence at Second Creek, an inquiry into a Civil war Slave Conspiracy* (Baton Rouge: Louisiana State University Press, 1993), p. 6.

5. Herbert Aptheker, *American Negro Slave Revolts* (New York: International Publishers, 1993), p. 150.

6. William L. Van Deburg, *Black Camelot* (Chicago: The University of Chicago Press, 1997), p. 2.

7. Diane Miller, national coordinator, Underground Network to Freedom, National Park Service, personal Interview, September 2001 and February 2003.

8. Diane Perrin Coon, personal interview, November 2001 and February 2003.

9. Miller.

→ G L O S S A R Y ←

ABOLITIONIST—A person who wants to stop slavery and works to end it.

AMERICAN COLONIZATION SOCIETY—Founded in 1816 for the purpose of advocating that free people be returned to Africa.

BACKLASH—A hostile reaction to a previous action.

BORDER STATES—Free states that bordered on slave states.

COMMANDEER—Seize for a military purpose.

EMANCIPATE—To set free.

FACTION—A group seeking to promote their own interests.

FREEMEN—African Americans who had been slaves.

FUGITIVE SLAVE—A person who was running away from slavery.

INDENTURED SERVANTS—Someone who is paying off a debt by working for a certain period of time.

INTEGRATE—Mixing races

MANUMITTED—A master legally freeing his/her slave.

MAROONS—Slaves who left the plantation and formed their own communities in the wilderness.

RACISM—Prejudice against certain groups or classes of people.

RACIST—Someone who is prejudiced.

SLAVE CODES—Laws governing how a slave should act or conduct themselves.

STATIONMASTER—A person who runs a stop on the Underground Railroad.

UNDERGROUND RAILROAD—A secret network of escape routes to help escaped slaves reach freedom.

FURTHER READING

Bentley, Judith. *"Dear Friend": Thomas Garrett & William Still, Collaborators on the Underground Railroad.* New York: Cobblehill Books, 1997.

Brackett, Virginia. *John Brown: Abolitionist.* Philadelphia: Chelsea House Publishers, 2001.

Burchard, Peter. *Frederick Douglass: For the Great Family of Man.* New York: Atheneum Books for Young Readers, 2003.

Fradin, Dennis Brindell. *Bound for the North Star: True Stories of Fugitive Slaves.* New York: Clarion Books, 2000.

Gregson, Susan R. *Nat Turner: Rebellious Slave.* Mankato, Minn.: Bridgestone Books, 2003.

Hansen, Joyce, and Gary McGowan. *Freedom Roads: Searching for the Underground Railroad.* Chicago: Cricket Books, 2003.

McDonough, Yona Zeldis. *Who Was Harriet Tubman?* New York: Grosset & Dunlap, 2002.

McKissack, Patricia C. and Frederick L. McKissack. *Rebels Against Slavery: American Slave Revolts.* New York: Scholastic, 1996.

Moore, Cathy. *The Daring Escape of Ellen Craft.* Minneapolis: Carolrhoda Books, 2002.

Myers, Walter Dean. *Amistad: A Long Road to Freedom.* New York: Dutton Children's Books, 1998.

Reef, Catherine. *This Our Dark Country: The American Settlers of Liberia.* New York: Clarion Books, 2002.

Swain, Gwenyth. *President of the Underground Railroad: A Story About Levi Coffin.* Minneapolis: Carolrhoda Books, 2001.

Unchained Memories: Readings From the Slave Narratives. Boston: Bulfinch Press, 2002.

INTERNET ADDRESSES

AFRICANS IN AMERICA: NAT TURNER'S REBELLION
<http://www.pbs.org/wgbh/aia/part3/3p1518.html>

DOCUMENTING THE AMERICAN SOUTH
<http://docsouth.unc.edu>

NATIONAL GEOGRAPHIC: THE UNDERGROUND RAILROAD
<http://www.nationalgeographic.com/features/99/railroad/>

HISTORIC SITES

THE FREDERICK DOUGLASS NATIONAL HISTORIC SITE
1411 W Street SE, Washington, D.C. 20020-4813
(202) 426-5961
<http://www.nps.gov/frdo/freddoug.html>

HARPERS FERRY NATIONAL HISTORIC PARK
P.O. Box 65, Harpers Ferry, West Virginia 25425
(304) 535-6298
<http://www.nps.gov/hafe/home.htm>

THE HARRIET TUBMAN HOME
180 South Street, Auburn, New York 13201
(315) 252-2081
E-mail: HTHome@localnet.com
<http://www.nyhistory.com/harriettubman/>

✦ INDEX ✦